THE BIG BOOK OF
UNEXPLAINED MYSTERIES

38 Mind-Boggling and Unsolved
Mysteries Through History

BILL O'NEILL

ISBN: 978-1-64845-087-7

DON'T FORGET YOUR FREE BOOKS

Get it on www.Triviabill.com

CONTENTS

INTRODUCTION

One of the things that make our world so wonderful and interesting is its many mysteries. Since the dawn of human civilization more than 5,000 years ago, philosophers, scientists, and theologians have sought to understand how and why things work - and many mysteries have been solved over the years.

For instance, just over 100 years ago, two brave men solved the riddle of flight, and just before that, others uncovered the secrets of electricity, light, radio, and a host of other technological mysteries. And other, stranger mysteries have also been solved throughout the millennia.

Ancient dead languages, such as the Egyptian and the Maya hieroglyphic scripts, have been deciphered and translated, lost cities have been found, and notorious crime mysteries have been solved.

But, of course, there remain hundreds of unexplained mysteries of all types in the world. In *The Big Book of Unexplained Mysteries*, you'll be introduced to 43 of the strangest, seemingly unsolvable mysteries the world has ever known.

You'll read about mysterious lost treasures, such as the ancient Germanic warlord Alaric's tomb and the possible location of King Solomon's mines. Strange science mysteries are also covered, including the mysterious hexagon on Saturn and the bizarre blobs that fell on Oakville, Washington in 1994.

When it comes to unexplained mysteries, this book truly has something for everyone -history, science, the supernatural, and true crime - so I guarantee that whatever your interests are, they're sure to be covered in this book!

So, buckle up, strap in, and get ready for a ridiculous ride through 43 of the strangest mysteries known to humanity... if you dare!

ZANA THE WILD WOMAN

If you had to point to one country in the world that's a bit mysterious by its nature, Russia would be a good pick. Its vastness puts it in both Europe and Asia, but in many ways, culturally, it's in neither.

Rugged mountain ranges, raging rivers, and remote forests isolate large pockets of Russians from the rest of the world.

And in the southern central portion of Russia, where it abuts smaller countries that were once part of the Soviet Union, the physical and cultural isolation is even more pronounced. Such as in the Republic of Abkhazia.

In case you're wondering where Abkhazia is, don't feel alone - I had to look it up myself! It's a small country in the Caucasus Mountains that borders on the Black Sea, just south of Russia and north of Georgia. Georgia actually claims it as a province, but that's a story for another book. What brings us to Abkhazia is an anthropological mystery that began in the 1850s that continues to the present.

It was during the 1850s when villagers in the remote Ochamchira district began reporting seeing a "wild woman" in the mountains

3

and hills. The physical descriptions of her can only be described as incredible.

She was said to be 6'6 and covered in hair from head to toe. The wild woman, who later was named Zana, was also said to have been able to outrun horses, easily pick up logs, and could swim across raging mountain rivers. As strange as this mystery is, though, it only gets more mysterious.

The men in the village near where Zana spent most of her time organized a posse to track down and capture the wild woman. She apparently put up quite a fight, with it taking several men using clubs to subdue her and put her in a cage. The villagers later dug a trench around her cage and lined it with spikes to prevent her from leaving.

Zana was eventually tamed enough that she became a sort of pet for a local noble who would show her off to his friends.

According to the reports, Zana slept outside, hated heated rooms, and enjoyed getting drunk on Georgian wine. Those who personally knew Zana claimed she was a human-ape hybrid and often referred to as an *almas*. Central Asian legends describe this ape-man type creature that lurks in the Caucasus and other mountain ranges, rarely coming into contact with humans.

But the problem with this theory is that Zana actually gave birth to children!

Yes, you read that correctly, men actually did copulate with Zana the Wild Woman. In fact, Zana gave birth to several children with several different men, although many of those children didn't live because she was known to wash them in the cold mountain rivers. Eventually, the locals took two of Zana's sons and two of her daughters away from her, successfully raising them and thereby proving that Zana was human. Many of those children had children whose descendants are known today.

Zana died in the 1890s and unfortunately the location of her grave is unknown, prohibiting further studies into what she was.

But what about her descendants?

Well, thanks to advances in DNA science, Oxford professor Bryan Sykes hoped he would be able to solve the mystery of Zana's origins once and for all. After testing the saliva of some of Zana's known ancestors, answers were finally thought to be at hand.

The DNA tests of her descendants show 100% African ancestry, but that finding seemed to raise more questions and create more mysteries than answers.

First, although the DNA test showed an African ancestry, she did not physically resemble any known African ethnic group. Unfortunately, there are no photographs of Zana, but based on eyewitness descriptions, she looked nothing like any African. Although Zana was described as having a dark complexion, her hair was straight and thick and dark reddish in color.

But even if Zana was African in the modern sense, that raises many questions.

How would an African have traveled to the remote region and why was she the only one? One popular answer to this was that she was an African woman who was enslaved by the Ottoman Turks and then escaped to the remote region where she was later found. Although it's true that the Ottomans did keep African slaves, we must go back to the original problem of her very un-African features.

Another theory is that Zana was a remnant of a Neanderthal population that survived extinction. Although the Neanderthals are believed to have become completely extinct about 30,000 to 40,000 years ago, the region where Zana was discovered was one of the core areas of Neanderthal culture, and it's technically possible for some Neanderthals to have survived the extinction. Plus, the descriptions of Zana's facial features fit perfectly with what Neanderthals are believed to have looked like.

But there are problems with this theory as well.

The description of Zana's facial features may have sounded Neanderthal, but at 6'6, she was nearly a foot and a half taller than the average Neanderthal female. There's also the obvious question of why other Neanderthals were not found if she was part of a breeding population.

The Neanderthals were a migratory people, so if a pocket of them did survive, it seems likely that more of them would have been seen and reported in that historical era.

So, while some of the questions about Zana's origins may have been answered, it appears that many others will forever remain a bizarre mystery.

MASS PSYCHOSIS OR ERGOT POISONING?

If you're ever traveling through southcentral France on your way to Monaco or other destinations in the Mediterranean, you may stop in the sleepy town of Pont-Saint-Esprit. It's a charming spot located on the Rhone River, but other than its country charm and old-world feel, it really isn't very famous.

No great cathedrals tower over the town and no major battles were ever fought there.

Unless you consider the events of August 15, 1951.

On that day, something truly bizarre - and so far, unexplained 0- gripped the residents of Pont-Saint-Esprit. Throughout that day, residents of the town were overwhelmed by an invisible hand of pandemonium that only seemed to worsen as the day progressed. For many of the residents of the town, it must have looked and felt like they truly were in the midst of a battle.

But it was an enemy they couldn't see or even identify.

The day began with several residents visiting the town's two doctors complaining of stomach aches, nausea, vomiting, and other flu-like and/or food poisoning type symptoms.

7

But then things got very strange.

Residents began reporting some wild hallucinations.

Pont-Saint-Esprit's postman at the time, Leon Armunier, recalled the following outlandish account.

"It was terrible. I had the sensation of shrinking and shrinking, and the fire and the serpents coiling around my arms."

After he fell off his bicycle and became what appeared to be a raging lunatic, the police took Armunier to an insane asylum in the nearby city of Avignon where he shared a room with three teenagers from Pont-Saint-Esprit who were experiencing similar, frightening hallucinations.

And as the day went on, the trip only got worse for Pont-Saint-Esprit.

There was a report of a man who jumped out the window of his house, broke his legs, and somehow got up and limped away. As that was happening, another man attempted to traverse the town's bridge over the Rhone River by tightrope walking on the bridge cables, because he believed he was a circus tightrope walker!

Numerous assaults were reported, with those committing the assaults, often on friends or family, believing that the people they were assaulting were demons or monsters. A young girl ran through the streets claiming she was being chased by tigers, while a man said he was being pursued by thieves with donkey ears.

There were even reports that the strange phenomena was also affecting animals. A dog reportedly chewed on rocks until it lost its teeth!

Despite the horror that many of the town's residents experienced on that day, some people apparently enjoyed the effects of whatever was afflicting everyone. A number of residents later reported feeling blissful, calm, and high. They also claimed to have seen a kaleidoscope of colors, heard wonderful music coming from the skies, and were suddenly inspired to be creative, philosophical, and thoughtful about the world.

But the results of the incident at Pont-Saint-Esprit were far from blissful for most. More than 250 people were reportedly affected, with 50 people interned into asylums and 7 dead. The incident was for the most part over by that evening, but then came the investigation into what, or who caused the mayhem.

The police almost immediately began focusing their attention on a local bakery, eventually concluding that a bag of flour tainted with ergot was the culprit. Ergot is a fungus that grows on yeast, and if ingested can produce food poisoning symptoms or have effects similar to those of an LSD/acid 'trip'. Ergot poisoning, commonly known as ergotism, was a not uncommon occurrence in Europe in the Middle Ages, but the last known case in France before 1951 was in 1816.

Opponents of the ergotism theory argue that the amount of ergot in the bread was very small and that ergot was often present in French bread at the time anyway. They claimed it couldn't have had such a massive effect on the people.

But something did make the people of Pont-Saint-Esprit experience something bizarre that day and if it wasn't ergot, what else could it have been?

Some have argued that it was mercury poisoning and that the water, not the bread, was the source.

Theories outside the mainstream include a sort of mass psychosis gripping the town, or even a portal of Hell being opened on that day.

But perhaps the most interesting theory involves a CIA document that was uncovered by journalist Hank Albarelli in 2009. The document reads:

"Re: Pont-Saint-Esprit and F. Olson Files. SO, Span/France Operation file, inclusive Olson. Intel files. Hand carry to Belin - tell him to see to it that these are buried."

The F. Olson mentioned is probably former CIA agent Frank Olson, who was one of the CIA's lead men at the time on the effects of LSD and other hallucinogenic drugs. It's now known that the CIA surreptitiously dosed unsuspecting civilians with acid and other hallucinogens in operations such as Project MK-Ultra and Operation Midnight Climax. As such, it's perhaps not a stretch to think that the incident at Pont-Saint-Esprit was a joint CIA-French intelligence operation that got a little out of control.

Or maybe it was just what they intended?

The attribution of the poisoning to the CIA in Albarelli's book has been roundly criticized. Historian Steven Kaplan, author of an earlier book about the events, said that this would be "clinically incoherent: LSD takes effects in just a few hours, whereas the inhabitants showed symptoms only after 36 hours or more. Furthermore, LSD does not cause the digestive ailments or the vegetative effects described by the townspeople."

Then again, maybe it really *was* a wacky form of mass psychosis?

VANISHING WORLD WAR I ACES

There's no doubt that war is an awful thing to experience. Cities and homes are physically destroyed, people are killed and maimed, and unmeasurable phycological scars are inflicted.

And many people simply vanish.

Most people who "vanish" during a war return to their homes at some point, usually suffering from post-traumatic stress disorder or having had amnesia. Among those who never return home, many were killed but never identified, while others went far from their homelands and began new lives with new identities.

But there are still a number of cases of people who vanished in wartime that remain unexplained and quite strange. Among the most notable is a cluster of World War I aces who flew their planes into oblivion in the last year of the war.

One of the most notable of these missing aces was Frenchman Georges Guynemer, who was an ace 18 times over (you "only" need to score three victories over enemy planes to be considered an ace), scoring an impressive 54 victories, which made him the second-most successful French ace when he went missing on September 11, 1917.

On that day, Guynemer reportedly flew into combat against a squadron of German planes and was never seen again.

German pilots captured by the Allies later claimed that Guynemer was shot in the head by one of their pilots - possibly none other than Baron von Richthofen, the "Red Baron," himself -and that his body and plane were taken away.

But other reports conflicted with the German accounts and, in the end, neither Guynemer's body nor his plane was ever recovered. This may not seem strange at first since it was war, but it is when you consider the nature of air warfare in World War I.

A possible source of information received by the Red Cross says Guynemer was shot through the head north of Poelcapelle, on the Ypres front. His body was identified by a photograph on his pilot's license found in his pocket. The burial took place at Brussels in the presence of a guard of honor, composed of the 5th Prussian Division. Such is the story told by a Belgian, who has just escaped from the Germans. The burial was about to take place at Poelcapelle, when the bombardment preceding the British attack at Ypres started. The burying party hastily withdrew, taking the body with them. The German General chanced to be an aviation enthusiast with a great admiration for Captain Guynemer's achievements. At his direction the body was taken to Brussels in a special funeral car. Thither the captain was carried by non-commissioned officers and was covered with floral tributes from German aviators. The Prussian Guards stood at salute upon its arrival and during the burial, which was given all possible military honors. The French Government has been invited to place in the Pantheon, where many great Frenchmen are buried, an inscription to perpetuate the memory of Captain Guynemer as 'a symbol of the aspirations and enthusiasm of the Army.' A resolution to this effect has been introduced in the Chamber of Deputies by Deputy Lasies.

One of the most unique aspects of World War I air warfare was the respect pilots on both sides showed for each other. Most of the European pilots were of the nobility and were, therefore, officers, so they followed rules of warfare that were influenced by earlier eras of history. The pilots knew who the aces were on the other side (pilots usually decorated their planes with unique markings) and when any pilot was captured, they were always given the best prisoner lodgings.

So, it's odd that the body and plane of an ace as well known as Guynemer was never recovered.

The second factor to take into consideration is the size and the out of the ordinary look of the planes at the time. Remember, the Wright Brothers only made their first flight in 1903, so when combat planes were buzzing over the Western Front in World War I, it must have been quite a sight to soldiers and civilians alike.

And when one went down, it would have been difficult to hide. Also, since World War I airplanes were slower and flew lower than later fighter planes, they were rarely incinerated when they crashed.

It should also be pointed out that all of these disappearances happened over land, so some signs of the plane wreckage would be expected.

Further, Guynemer was not the only ace to mysteriously vanish in World War I.

13

British ace Arthur Percival Foley Rhys-Davids was reportedly shot down by German fighters on October 27, 1917, but neither he nor his plane was recovered.

Note: On 27 October 1917 Rhys-Davids was promoted to lieutenant, backdated to 1 September 1917. That same day he took off on a routine patrol and was last seen flying east of Roeselare chasing a group of German Albatros fighters. The Luftstreitkräfte (German Air Service) credited Karl Gallwitz with shooting him down. It was not until 29 December 1917 that a report came through that a German aircraft had dropped a note to inform the RFC of Rhys-Davids' death.

Then there was the mysterious case of French ace Antoine Cordonnier, who left his base on July 28, 1918, never to be seen or heard from again.

Note: By the time he disappeared, he had won the Croix de Guerre with seven Palmes. On 3 August 1918, he was made a Chevalier of the Legion d'honneur.

British ace Herbert Gould suffered the same fate as the other aces, although he flew a two-seater, so he disappeared along with his gunner, Ewart William Frederick Jinman, on August 14, 1918.

Note: Gould was awarded the Military Cross, which was gazetted on 13 September, after his death. His citation read: For conspicuous gallantry and devotion to duty. He has carried out 24 successful bombing raids, several of which he has led, and 26 low reconnaissance and bombing flights, as well as many low-flying, harassing and bombing patrols, during which many direct hits have been obtained and severe casualties inflicted. He has destroyed three enemy machines and has shown a very high spirit of zeal throughout.

Of course, the simplest explanation for these disappearances is that they were all killed and their remains, and the remains of their planes, were either destroyed in land battles or simply overlooked. But you also can't help but wonder if perhaps something stranger was at work over the skies of Europe in the final months of World War I.

A BLOND HAIR BLUE EYE
SOUTH AMERICAN TRIBE?

When Europeans first began making contact with the natives of the New World in the 1500s, they encountered people they had never seen before. The physical looks, cultures, and mannerisms of the indigenous peoples of the Americas awed, mystified, and sometimes repulsed the Europeans, who quickly set out to conquer them.

Anthropologists believe that the Americas were initially peopled by migrants from Asia, who traveled across what was at the time a land bridge that connected Siberia and Alaska between 18,000 and 26,000 years ago, although it may have been as late as 15,000 years ago. So, genetically and physically speaking, many of these people the Europeans first met in the 1500s most closely resembled Asian peoples they had seen and heard about back in Eurasia (the name for the continuous landmass of Europe and Asia).

On the other hand, Europeans were quite a sight in the eyes of the indigenous Americans.

The indigenous Americans had never before seen people with blue eyes, red or blond hair, and fair complexions. The facial hair that most conquistadors would also have been quite strange to the indigenous peoples. It would have been the first time they saw people with these features…

Or maybe not.

When the Spanish, led by Francisco Pizarro and other conquistadors, began exploring and conquering South America in the 1500s, they met a diverse array of tribes with varying degrees of technological capabilities. The most advanced from the European perspective was the Inca of the Andes Mountains. By the time the Spanish had arrived in the region in the early 1500s, the Inca had built great cities, developed a sophisticated culture, and conquered most of their neighbors.

The Spanish were truly impressed with the Inca and their neighbors. Many of the conquistadors took the time to write down their observations of the Inca - at least when they weren't killing them and conquering their empire!

One of the most mysterious and still unexplained observations was made by a Spanish military officer named Pedro Cieza de Leon. He described meeting a tribe known as the *Chachapoya,* which was a Quechua (the language of the Inca) word meaning "cloud people." The Chachapoya developed a sophisticated culture in the 9th century CE on the eastern slope of the Andes Mountains that included cities and stone monuments. The Chachapoya were also known as a warrior people, but they were not warlike enough to keep from being conquered by the ever-expanding Inca Empire in 1475.

All of this impressed Leon, but even more was the Chachapoyas' physical appearance. He later wrote in his book about the Spanish conquest of the Inca:

"They are the whitest and most handsome of all the people that I have seen in Indies, and their wives were so beautiful that because of their gentleness, many of them deserved to be the Incas' wives and to also be taken to the Sun Temple."

Another Spanish conquistador named Pedro Pizarro was also quoted as saying that all the Chachapoya were white and had blond hair. Other conquistadors of the mid-1500s described the Chachapoya similarly.

So, how was it possible for a European/White tribe to inhabit South America long before the first Europeans supposedly arrived in the region?

The answer to this question is not simple and there have been few reasonable explanations offered. Many scholars believe that Leon's use of the word "white" has been taken out of context since the racial classification terms we use today weren't in use at the time. Other scholars have also pointed out that Leon's writing was the only true first-hand account of the Chachapoya; the other accounts of the White Chachapoya were actually second-hand accounts that were written several years later.

All of this may be true, but it doesn't explain why Leon specifically noted that the Chachapoya had a notably lighter complexion than their neighbors.

If we accept that the Chachapoya were lighter with blond hair and blue eyes, then we are left looking for answers.

As we'll see in two other stories in this book, there is evidence that suggests people from Asia and Europe may have visited the Americas during the historical period. Could the Chachapoya have been the remnants of a Roman, Phoenician, or Norse expedition that was blown off course?

Possibly…

Or maybe the Chachapoya were a blond people when they crossed the land bridge between Siberia and Alaska and when they eventually made it to South America, their gene pool remained isolated.

Less likely but still possible.

The Chachapoya were eventually decimated by diseases brought by the Spanish and policies that forced the tribe into villages, but the mystery of their origins and physical appearance continues to intrigue millions of people around the world.

THE GREAT WRECKING
BALL HEIST

One of the key elements of any unexplained tale, and something that you've probably already noticed so far in this book, is that each of these stories takes on a life of its own. They're all very strange by any measure, but how and when they become "unexplained" is often a matter of perspective and degrees. Yes, some of these stories are truly unexplainable and will remain so for eternity, while others may have had a logical explanation that's been lost due to a combination of hype and misreporting.

Our next case falls into this category, although it's no less strange than any of the others we profile in this book. It made the rounds for many years in articles, books, and documentaries about the unexplained and unsolved. Although it's not apparently supernatural - at least, it doesn't *seem* to be - it's worthy of an entry in our book of unexplained mysteries.

On July 17, 1973, when workers of the Dowling Construction Company reported for work to demolish a building in Indianapolis, Indiana, they were mystified to find that the five-ton wrecking ball they had been using was missing.

Somehow, the wrecking ball that was suspended from a crane 20 feet above the Boy's Club it was demolishing, someone, or something, took it in the middle of the night.

The construction company's owner, Loren Dowling, told a local newspaper:

"I can't figure out what someone would do with a five-ton metal ball."

Well, neither can most people, which has caused skeptics to ask several questions about this unsolved mystery. It even earned an entry in the 1982 book, *Mysteries of the Unexplained.*

The most plausible theory is that the thieves, probably employees of the company, simply pulled a truck under the ball, lowered the ball onto the truck, and then drove it away. The thieves then sold the ball as scrap and pocketed a nice little profit.

That sounds logical enough, but there are a few holes in the theory. First, no witnesses reported hearing or seeing anything that night. You would think that the theft of something so big would be seen or heard by someone, right?

Second, there were no reports of the ball being sold to local scrapyards. Of course, the thieves could've sold it to a scrapyard farther away, or melted it down themselves, but the sudden disappearance of something so large is certainly more than a little strange.

So, that leaves us looking for other explanations.

There are a few other theories that may explain what is otherwise unexplainable in this case. The first is that the report was simply wrong. The *Indianapolis Star* published a follow-up report one day later that stated the wrecking ball was in fact stolen, but that it was only 50 pounds, not five tons. This would certainly explain how the wrecking ball was stolen without anyone knowing about it, but the explanation doesn't take into account one simple and obvious fact - wrecking balls have to be much larger than 50 pounds!

Another more mundane explanation is that the story was totally made up by Dowling to collect insurance money. The problem with this theory, though, is that the case was fully investigated by the local authorities, there was plenty of media scrutiny, and no signs of fraud were ever detected.

A fraud like that likely would have involved multiple people, and since it became a fairly well-reported case in the local press, someone would have eventually talked, right?

But no one ever did.

So, that leaves more out-of-this-world explanations for this bizarre heist. At this point, you can let your imagination run wild because when you're dealing with the unexplained like we are, anything is possible!

THE LOST CITY OF PAITITI

The Inca people of the Andes Mountains range in South America built an amazingly, stable state that lasted for more than 400 years. The Inca Empire began in the 1100s when a small group of Quechua speaking people founded the city of Cusco/Cuzco in what is today Peru.

From there the Inca Empire grew, as the well-organized and militaristic Inca conquered their neighbors and built new cities (most notably Manchu Pichu), roads, and monuments. Its vast size included nearly all of the modern nation-state of Peru and parts of Bolivia, Ecuador, Colombia, Argentina, and Chile.

But as great as the Inca Empire was, it couldn't withstand the guns and disease brought by Francisco Pizarro and his band of conquistadors. After capturing the Sapa Inca (Inca king) Atahualpa on November 16, 1532, the Spanish had conquered the Inca Empire. The Spanish crushed the final embers of Inca resistance in 1572, giving them complete control of one of the New World's most advanced cultures.

The Spanish were largely driven by greed in their conquest, particularly control of South America's rich gold and silver deposits. And as the Spanish discovered more and more of these deposits, they also began to hear stories of the lost Inca cities that were filled with gold.

The lost city that intrigued them the most was called Paititi.

There are two sources for the legendary city of Paititi: local/native and Spanish. Let's start with the local legends.

According to one, a legendary, semi-mythical person named Inkarri first founded Q'ero and Cusco, and then retired to the hidden city of Pantiacolla (Paititi). There are different variations of this legend, but nearly all place the location of Paititi somewhere east of the Andes Mountains in the jungles on the western edge of the Amazonian Basin.

The local legends of Paititi are complicated by the nature of Incan record keeping. Although the Inca never developed writing, they did create a unique form of record-keeping called *quipu*. The quipu system involved tying different colored knotted strings together. The various colors, lengths of the strings, and knots all represented different values. Modern scholars know that the Inca used the quipu for accounting purposes, but some believe the strings may also have been used phonetically as a type of proto-writing.

If this is true, then the mystery of Paititi could be solved by a quipu, but in the meantime, adventurers will have to look elsewhere for answers.

A possible breakthrough in this mystery came in 2001 when Italian archaeologist Mario Polia discovered a report from the early 1600s that was written by a Jesuit named Andres Lopez. The account describes a fantastic city that's filled with gold and other treasures, hidden deep in the jungle far from where any treasure hunters would find it.

A number of other reports of possible sightings of the city from the 1500s through the 1700s placed the lost city in the same region, but it was never definitively located. After that period, though, interest in Paititi declined.

By the late 1800s, a new generation of European and North American explorers was fanning out across the globe in search of treasures and lost cities. When they began hearing the local legends of Paititi, a number of these men thought they'd try their luck at finding it.

One of the earliest expeditions to try to find Paititi was undertaken by a former Nazi filmmaker named Hans Ertl in 1954-55. Although Ertl's expedition was unsuccessful, it inspired a plethora of expeditions to find Paititi over the following 60 years, including a 2014 "attempt" by American TV personality Josh Gates.

From the beginning, efforts to locate Paititi have been primarily undertaken by non-academics, which has at times only added to the legend of the city and resulted in some pretty fantastic claims.

In 2016, Frenchman Vincent Pélissier claimed on his YouTube channel that he had, at last, discovered the lost city of Paititi. Pélissier said that the Petroglyphs of Pusharo, which are located in Peru's Manu National Park, point the way to the lost city.

Despite the ancient map, plenty of new technology, and Pélissier's bold claim, Paititi's location remains unknown.

If it even exists.

The location, or existence, of the lost city of Paititi will likely remain a mystery for the foreseeable future, so if you have a large spirit of adventure, some money, and can speak Spanish, maybe you can be the one to get to the bottom of it.

SHARK OR SEA MONSTER?

Our planet's oceans are quite vast, covering 70.8% of the Earth's surface or 139,000,000 square miles.

And that's just the surface.

The depths of the oceans are equally as vast. For example, the maximum depth of the Marianna Trench in the Pacific Ocean has been measured at just over 36,037 (±) feet, or about 7,000 feet deeper than Mount Everest is high!

So with all that area and depth, you shouldn't be surprised that fishermen and scientists find some strange things in the ocean from time to time, especially since they are comparatively underexplored.

In 1938, a fisherman caught a coelacanth off the coast of South Africa. Normally, the catch wouldn't be a big deal, other than the fish being quite large and ugly, but because the coelacanth was believed to have gone extinct 65 to 66 million years earlier, it was quite the find. The coelacanth's discovery meant that biology books had to be rewritten and scholars had to ask what else may be lurking beneath the ocean.

Note: What is so special about the coelacanth? Unique to any other living animal, the coelacanth has an intracranial joint, a hinge in its skull that allows it to open its mouth extremely wide to consume large prey. Instead of a backbone, they have a notochord. Coelacanths retain an oil-filled notochord, a hollow, pressurized tube that serves as a backbone.

Less than 40 years later, on April 25, 1977, marine biologists were faced with another mysterious anomaly when a Japanese fisherman onboard the *Zuiyō-maru* caught something in their nets that still has people in awe.

The day began like any other for the fishermen, as they were chasing a school of mackerel about 30 miles off the shore from Christchurch, New Zealand. The crew pulled up their net and were shocked to find the carcass of something none of them had ever seen before.

It appeared to have a long neck, large pectoral fins, and a long tail. It measured 33 feet long and weighed two tons. The carcass gave off a terrible odor, and since it wasn't something that the crew could sell for food, whatever it was, they decided to throw it back into the ocean. But before they did, crewman Michihiko Yano took five photos of the bizarre catch. Pieces of the flesh were also kept.

When the crew returned to Japan, Yano's photos quickly made the rounds in the Japanese media and eventually the world media.

Academics and lay people alike were amazed by the photos, with many thinking it was proof that dinosaurs still lived among us. They argued that it was probably a plesiosaur; or some other

28

creature that had been thought to have been extinct since the Jurassic period. Others took this line of reasoning even a step further by arguing that the *Zuiyō-maru* carcass was proof that the Loch Ness Monster was real.

The initial media and popular frenzy after the *Zuiyō-maru* was discovered was elevated when Yano produced a sketch of what he believed the mystery creature looked like. Yano's rendition was clearly a plesiosaur, which was taken by many to be more proof that dinosaurs still swim in the oceans.

Japanese academics, such as Professor Yoshinori Imaizumi, director of animal research at Tokyo National Science Museum, believed it was a plesiosaur, while American and European scholars were skeptical.

The skeptics said that as strange as the carcass looked, it resembled that of a basking shark.

The Taiyo Fish Company, which owned the *Zuiyō-maru*, conducted tests on samples of what they said was flesh from the creature. The skeptics felt justified when the results showed an amino acid profile similar to that of modern sharks.

But not so fast, screamed the pro-plesiosaur crowd. They argued that just because the flesh sample showed a similar amino acid profile to modern sharks it doesn't necessarily disqualify if from having a similar profile to another animal as well. Besides, who's to say that the sample the Taiyo Fish Company used was really from the mystery creature?

A DNA sample would conceivably solve the question, but there is no surviving sample of the flesh.

Those who believe the carcass was that of something other than a shark also make a few other important points. The fishermen reported that the carcass smelled more like a dead marine animal than a rotting shark, and they also claimed that they saw no dorsal fin.

The skeptics will quickly retort that that dorsal fin was gone because it had rotted away.

But that leaves the final and perhaps most important question of this mystery. If the carcass was that of a rotting basking shark, as the skeptics claim, why are there no other known similar pictures of shark carcasses? If this was a common pattern of basking shark decomposition, there would be plenty of other photographs of this phenomenon, right?

TUNNELING INTO A BANK AND GETTING AWAY WITH MILLIONS

The old adage, "crime doesn't pay," is true for the most part. The average career criminal usually spends the majority of his life behind bars and usually never gets to retire with any of his ill-gotten gains. What the career criminal doesn't spend on booze, drugs, or women is usually confiscated by the authorities.

Then there are those rare cases where a criminal, or a group of criminals, put together the heist of the century. One where they never have to commit another crime and can quietly retire to a South American country.

But *Ocean's 11* was just a movie, right?

Well, there have been some very rare, very successful heists. So successful, in fact, that they warrant being added to the pages of this book on the world's greatest unexplained mysteries. This next case makes our list due to all the questions that still surround it.

The authorities know the general outline and details of what happened, such as how the thieves pulled it off, how much money they took, and a couple of the leaders of the crew. But

31

many of the details remain, and apparently will always remain, a mystery.

This mystery began on December 14, 1932, when Albert "Bert" Spaggiari was born in southeastern France. Young Spaggiari personally experienced the turmoil of World War II and lived under the pro-Nazi Vichy government.

The experiences had quite the effect on Spaggiari, as he enlisted in the army and became an elite paratrooper.

Spaggiari fought in the First Indochina War, in what is now Vietnam, and would have returned to France a hero, but he was a bit of a rebel who was drawn to the criminal lifestyle. He engaged in a series of crimes and was eventually arrested, tried, and convicted of armed robbery. After serving four years in prison for the crime, Spaggiari drifted around Europe and North Africa for a few years, making contacts in organized crime, right-wing paramilitaries such as the OAS (Secret Armed Organization), and numerous intelligence agencies.

Spaggiari eventually settled down in rural southern France, married, and opened a photography studio in Nice, but it's a mystery how he got the money for his lifestyle.

Well, probably not much of a mystery. He was quite an accomplished criminal.

On the weekend of Bastille Day 1976, Spaggiari and a number of accomplices tunneled into the safe deposit box vault in the Société Générale bank in Nice. The evidence shows that the crew spent two months digging a 26-foot-long tunnel from the sewers up through the bottom of the vault. Once they got in, the thieves welded the vault door from the inside so they could take their time emptying the vault. The crew hauled an estimated 50 million francs worth of loot, which is the equivalent of about €29 million.

The thieves even had a nice French meal while they took several days emptying the vault! Before leaving, the thieves scrawled the message *sans armes, ni haine, ni violence* ("without weapons, hatred, or violence").

Although the police could immediately see *how* the thieves pulled the heist off, the mystery was they didn't know *who* did it. But within a few days, Spaggiari's name came up, leading to his arrest. It seemed as though the mystery of the tunnel heist would soon be over, and all the players and loot would be located. However, like a true career criminal, Spaggiari kept his mouth shut.

Then this mysterious case quickly became even more mysterious.

When Spaggiari was brought to court in 1977, he had his lawyer introduce a coded document as evidence. As the judge attempted to read the unreadable piece of paper, Spaggiari jumped through a window and onto the hood of a car. He then jumped onto the back of a motorcycle and was whisked away.

Over the next 12 years, Spaggiari was spotted in Argentina, Chile, France, and Italy, but the authorities were always one step behind. It is believed that Spaggiari's extensive criminal, political, and intelligence connections kept him free, but they couldn't keep him alive.

Spaggiari is said to have died from cancer on June 8, 1989, in Italy, but for years it was believed that he died under mysterious circumstances. And there are some who claim that Spaggiari lived for many years after 1989.

Spaggiari's share of the loot was never recovered. It's possible that it is hidden somewhere, waiting to be found, but it's more likely that he spent it on fake IDs and traveling the world to say ahead of the police.

So, most of the mysteries of the Nice's great sewer heist are solved, right?

Not exactly!

This mysterious case took a new turn in 2010, when a man from Marseille named Jacques Cassandri claimed he was the true mastermind of the sewer heist. Cassandri, who has ties to the Corsican mafia, wrote a fictional book under a pen name stating that he, not Spaggiari, had led the brazen thieves into the Société Générale vault.

Cassandri was wise enough to publish his book after the statute of limitations were up on the 'Nice heist', but the now elderly crook was hit with many other charges, including money laundering and tax evasion.

There are still several unanswered questions about this heist that will likely ensure that it stays one of the top true-crime mysteries of all time. How many others were involved and who were they? Knowing Spaggiari's background, they probably came from a number of different organizations and like him, they've all stayed mum.

Perhaps the most intriguing questions surround what happened to the loot. Cassandri apparently invested his share in legitimate businesses, but it's anyone's guess what happened to the other thieves' hauls.

None of the loot has ever been recovered.

A REAL-LIFE BLOB

During the 1950s, there was an endless parade of exceptionally bad sci-fi films. Most of these films were hampered by a combination of poor special effects due to the technical limitations of the era and the fact that the science they depicted was little understood by most people at the time. But, despite all this, some of these films became hits.

The 1958 sci-fi film, *The Blob*, featured the story of a meteorite that crashed in a rural area of Pennsylvania and unleashed a blob of gelatin that enveloped every living thing in its path. Other than being film legend Steve McQueen's first leading role, *The Blob* is often remembered as yet another cheesy '50s sci-fi flick that got all the science wrong.

Or did it?

On August 7, 1994, the residents of Oakville, Washington, population 493 in 1990, were greeted with a bizarre and sickening - literally - sight of thousands of clear, gelatinous blobs coming down with the rain, covering their lawns, houses, and cars.

The blobs covered 20 square miles of Oakville and the surrounding area in rural Grays Harbor County, Washington.

Local residents were perplexed at what they were witnessing, with many scooping bits of it up to examine what it was.

Local police officer David Lacey noted that it covered cars and windshield wipers were unable to remove it. "It's almost like if you had Jell-O in your hand and you could pretty much squish it through your fingers. We did have some bells go off in your heads that basically said that this isn't right, this isn't normal."

Lacey reported that he later became quite sick. "I started to put it together that whatever the substance was, it made me violently sick like I never had been before, to the point where it just totally shut me down."

Many others in the town who also reported touching the blobs also became sick, including Dotty Hearn and her daughter, Sunny Barclift.

The mysterious blob rain continued to fall on Oakville six more times over six weeks, prompting some national attention and a spot on the hit TV show *Unsolved Mysteries*.

Samples of the blobs were tested by professionals, beginning with a local hospital lab tech who found human white blood cells in the sample. More samples were then sent to the state medical lab, where a microbiologist from the Washington State Department of Health tested the blobs and found that they contained two types of terrestrial bacteria.

This meant that, unlike the blob Steve McQueen fought, the Oakville blobs definitely were from Earth. But that still left the mystery of what they were exactly, and even more intriguing: how did they come from the sky?

One seemingly credible theory is that they were human waste that had been dropped from an airplane. That would certainly explain why people got sick after touching the blobs, and the gelatinous texture may have been the result of the chemicals used to treat the waste.

So, local officials contacted the FAA about this possibility but were told it was highly unlikely since airlines dye human waste blue. The FAA didn't indicate, though, that planes *weren't* allowed to dump their waste in friendly skies!

Another potential explanation may be connected to the increased military activity local residents reported just before and during the blob rain. Numerous planes and helicopters, notably the ever-mysterious "black helicopters," were seen flying over Oakville numerous times. This led some residents to believe the blobs were the result of either a military-science experiment or the remains of jellyfish that were killed during a training exercise, carried into the atmosphere somehow, and then returned to the earth with rain.

Finally, it should be pointed out that what happened in Oakville wasn't unique and is actually a phenomenon that has been observed around the world throughout history.

The phenomenon of goo and other slimy stuff from the heavens that has mysteriously landed on earth is generally referred to as "star jelly." Some cases of star jelly have been identified as algae and fungus, but other samples have yielded no DNA, leaving several of these cases as legitimate mysteries.

It appears that the mystery of the Oakville blobs will remain so for the near future. Just remember that if you ever find your lawn or car covered by these things, use some caution and latex gloves when removing them.

THE CHINESE DISCOVERY
OF NORTH AMERICA

We're told from a young age that history is unchangeable and that it's "written in stone." But the truth is that archaeologists, anthropologists, and historians are constantly learning new things about the past and, therefore, are constantly rewriting the history books.

For example, Christopher Columbus is generally thought to be the first Old World explorer to have discovered the Americas. Most of us over the age of 45 were taught this in school and there are even "Columbus Day" celebrations in many countries.

But over time this "fact" was proven to be untrue. Scholars eventually demonstrated that the Norse/Vikings were in North America about 500 years before Columbus set foot on the warm sandy beaches of the Caribbean. Over the last few decades, several new theories about the Pre-Columbian exploration of the Americas have been put forward by many different individuals.

Some of these theories are a bit strange, while others have some definite merit. All of them represent mysteries of history that if solved, could drastically change the history books. We'll take a look at three of these mysterious theories in this book, beginning with the potential Chinese discovery of North America.

Former chemistry teacher and current independent scholar, John Ruskamp, has recently made the bold claim that he has proof the Chinese visited the American southwest in the ancient era. Ruskamp argues that some of the petroglyphs at the Petroglyph National Monument in Albuquerque, New Mexico are identical to Chinese characters used in the oracle bone writing of the Shang Dynasty (founded c. 1766-1027 BCE: writing began c. 1500 BCE) and that it proves the Chinese were here circa 1300 BCE.

Ruskamp offers no other evidence beyond the glyphs, only stating that he believes the Chinese who supposedly left the inscriptions were travelers who were blown off course and/or left behind by a larger group. Skeptics believe the glyphs were a form of writing that "was started" by local indigenous people and then stopped for some reason.

But that argument isn't very convincing either. Although there are plenty of examples of "dead" written languages in history, it is almost unheard of for people to develop a written language and then suddenly stop using it.

So, let's just file that away for now.

Another strange piece of evidence for the Pre-Columbian Chinese voyages to the Americas comes from the *Book of Liang*, which was compiled by a historian named Yao Silian in CE 635. The book describes a mysterious land called Fusang that is 20,000 li or about 6,666 miles to the east of China. This distance, of course, would put Fusang in the Americas, leading many to believe that it is proof the Chinese visited the land before turning around and heading back to Asia.

More proposed evidence for the Chinese discovery of America includes three donut-shaped rocks that were discovered by Chinese fishermen off the coast of California in 1973 and 1975. These stones were originally thought to be ancient Chinese anchors but testing later revealed they were made from local stone.

Yet this doesn't mean that pre-Columbian Chinese sailors couldn't have made the anchors locally and then left them behind when they returned to Asia.

Finally, the most colorful and perhaps least credible entry into the list of evidence for the Chinese discovery of North America was given by Gavin Menzies, a former British submarine commander turned popular historian.

Menzies claimed in his 2002 book, *1421: The Year China Discovered the World* that a Chinese expedition led by Zheng He (1371-1433/35) arrived in the New World in 1421 and then went on to circumnavigate the globe nearly 100 years before the Magellan Expedition.

Menzies based his claims on circumstantial evidence. Zeng He was a great mariner, merchant, and naval commander of the Ming Dynasty, who led "treasure voyages" for the Yongle Emperor to southeast Asia, the Middle East, and East Africa. However, there is no evidence that he crossed the Pacific Ocean. Zeng He led seven well-documented expeditions between 1405 and 1433, yet they were all to the south and all done to project Chinese power, not as exploratory expeditions.

So, what can be made of the mystery of the Chinese discovery of North America? It seems there are enough tidbits of intriguing information here and there to keep things interesting but not enough to prove anything one way or another. For the skeptics, there just isn't enough evidence; for the believers, all the pieces add up to the Chinese being in North America long before Columbus.

Until more solid evidence is found, though, the question of whether pre-Columbian Chinese explorers visited the Americas will remain an unexplained mystery.

WHAT HAPPENED TO WILLIAM SHARKEY?

Today approximately 600,000 people go missing every year in the United States, and although the vast majority of those cases are quickly solved, more than 17,000 of those cases remain open. Often, we never hear from those 17,000 unfortunate souls again, as they are often caught up in drug or alcohol addiction.

Their disappearances are usually much more tragic than they are mysterious.

But a number of those missing person cases are true unexplained mysteries and remain so until the present. Some of these missing persons disappeared under bizarre circumstances, leaving behind only a few clues that allow us to potentially track them down and unravel the secrets they may have once held. And some of these missing persons were colorful characters or important people during their lives, so their disappearances received greater than average media attention.

The case of William Sharkey is one such mystery.

In the late 1860s and early 1870s, William Sharkey seemingly had the world in the palm of his hands. While still in his early 20s,

Sharkey rose to prominence in the New York City political machine known as Tammany Hall. Sharkey came from a solid upper-class family in the city's Eighth Ward, but due to the state of politics at the time, a political career meant dipping his toes into the criminal underworld.

Tammany Hall was as corrupt as any political organization at the time, or today, although you could argue that the corruption, graft, and fraud practiced by Tammany politicians was more "honest" because they were much more open about it than modern politicians.

Everyone in New York City, as well as those throughout the country who followed politics, knew that Tammany Hall was a dirty political machine that wasn't afraid to race its opponents into the metaphorical political sewer by using a variety of tactics.

One of the unique features of Tammany Hall's corruption was recruiting gang members from the streets of Manhattan. Tammany politicians courted predominantly Irish gangs such as the Dead Rabbits for protection against nativist gangs like the Bowery Boys, more or less acting as paramilitary groups for the Democrat Party. Despite being upper-class, William Sharkey ran a gang known as the Sharkey Guard, which helped him gain entry into the Tammany Hall machine.

Sharkey used his connections on the streets to make inroads in the political arena, but politics is always a tough and dirty business. After Sharkey won the nomination for Assistant Alderman, for reasons that remain a mystery, the Tammany Hall machine threw Sharkey under the bus and cost him the election.

So, Sharkey returned to what he knew best, crime and gambling.

Sharkey's big plan was to make money playing faro in Buffalo, New York in 1872. Apparently, Sharkey thought that the rubes up in Buffalo would be easy marks for a big city guy like himself.

It's worth noting here that faro was a popular gambling card game in the 1800s that fell out of favor because its players were notorious for cheating.

Sharkey believed he could use the ability to cheat in faro to his advantage against the upstate hicks, but instead, he became their victim!

After losing more than $4000, Sharkey staked a professional gambler and city employee named Robert S. Dunn $600 to go up to Buffalo and win his money back.

Dunn was also either cleaned out in Buffalo, or he took the money and ran. The two men later saw each other at the funeral of a politician, where Sharkey found out Dunn had plenty of money, but he wasn't willing to share any of it.

Sharkey shot and killed Dunn out of anger and then surrendered to the police on September 1, 1872.

Now the story gets a whole lot more interesting and mysterious.

Sharkey awaited his trial in the notorious jail known as The Tombs. His lawyer argued for a manslaughter conviction, but Sharkey was convicted of premediated murder on June 21, 1873, and then on July 3, 1873, was sentenced to hang; but he won a temporary appeal.

As Sharkey fought his case on appeal, he stayed in The Tombs, but the accounts of the conditions of his stay there vary. According to one *New York Times* article, he was violent and placed in solitary confinement, while another article stated that he had a nice setup in his cell with plenty of booze.

I guess it could've been both.

The setup Sharkey had in his cell allowed what happened next to take place and for this once aspiring politician and career criminal to achieve immortality as an unsolved mystery.

On November 22, 1873, Sharkey received a visit in his cell from his girlfriend, Maggie Jourdan, and another woman named Sarah Allen. Apparently, the guards weren't watching them very closely - or maybe they were in on it - because, during the visit, Sharkey switched clothing with Allen and walked out of the prison with her pass.

There were reports of a stocky "woman" in a dress leaving The Tombs that day, but no one bothered to stop "her" to see what was happening. By the time the guards knew what had happened, Sharkey was long gone.

Sharkey went on the lam, but his movements remain largely remain a mystery even to this day.

He probably left New York in late 1873 or early 1874 and landed in Cuba. Jourdan joined Sharkey briefly in Cuba in 1876, where the couple married, but she returned to the States shortly after, apparently tired of living a life on the run.

After that, the details of Sharkey's life are sketchy at best.

One account describes that he worked as a spy for the Spanish government in Cuba, but that he ran into problems there and had to leave the island. Knowing what we know about Sharkey's criminal background, and his tendency to run afoul of those in power, this is certainly believable.

But where he went after Cuba only adds to this mystery.

One report claimed that Sharkey possibly went to South America in the 1890s and joined the military of a country there, but there's no corroborating evidence to support this notion. Joining the army seems a bit out of character for Sharkey, since doing so would have subjected him to a highly disciplined lifestyle.

If Sharkey went to South America, it is more likely that he did so to pull some scams or gamble than to join an army.

The final possible sighting of Sharkey was reported in a 1900 article of the *Auckland Star*, which stated that he was living in southern Spain and working as a tour guide. Sharkey would have been in his early 50s by that time (he was born sometime around 1847), so it's not unreasonable to think after learning Spanish during his Cuban sojourn that he ended up in the mother country of Spain.

Sharkey's trail went cold after the Spain sighting. Maybe William Sharkey lived out his final years in relative comfort with a new family and group of friends in Spain. Or maybe he died a wealthy man in Argentina or Uruguay. Or possibly he never left Cuba, having met the same fate he dished out to Dunn years earlier.

THE MISSING ROMANOV JEWELS

Perhaps one of the most intriguing, and most fun, categories of unexplained mysteries we examine in this book is lost fortunes and treasures. The obvious mystery surrounding all of these missing fortunes is where they are, but other minor mysteries accompany many of them, including how they were lost, the amount lost, and if the treasure even truly exists.

This unexplained mystery begins in 1918; well actually, it begins long before that year in many ways.

In 1918, the communist faction known as the Bolsheviks had taken control of Russia and they had the Russian royal family - Tsar Nicholas Romanov II, his wife Alexandra Feodorovna, their four daughters Olga, Tatiana, Maria, and Anastasia, and their son, Alexei - placed on house arrest in the city of Yekaterinburg.

During the late-night and early morning hours of July 16-17, a crew of Bolsheviks herded the Romanov family and their servants into a basement and brutally shot, stabbed, and beat them all to death. The Russian monarchy was quickly ended but almost immediately a modern mystery began.

The Romanovs' bodies were brought to a remote location where they were buried in an unmarked mass grave. The bodies were actually moved more than once, and as the communists were moving the bodies, they noticed that all the Romanov women, except Maria, had jewels sewed into their girdles.

So began the first part of the mystery of the missing Romanov treasure.

When the royalist forces briefly retook Yekaterinburg in 1919, they found evidence of the massacre of the royal family but were never able to locate the bodies. Royal investigator Nikolai Sokolov found some of the Romanov family jewels, but the vast majority were by that time long gone.

And the jewelry that the Romanov women had on them when they were killed was only a portion of the "crown jewels."

The "Russian Crown Jewels," as they were called, included elaborate diadems, necklaces, rings, crowns, brooches, medals, scepters, globes, as well as the more "common" jewelry the Romanov girls had on them when they were murdered. The complete collection of jewelry was amassed from the beginning of the Romanov Dynasty in 1613 until the Romanovs were removed from power in 1917.

The murder of the Romanovs took place during great turmoil, including the Russian Civil War, which lasted until June 16, 1923. When the smoke finally cleared, the obvious question on many people's minds was: where are the Russian Royal Jewels?

Unfortunately, no complete inventory of the jewels was ever recorded, which has led to many conspiracy theories about the location of some of the jewels and the entire situation becoming a legitimate unexplained and unsolved mystery.

So, let's start with what we know - well, sort of know!

Rumors almost immediately began circulating claiming that surviving members of the extended royal family took their shares of the jewels with them to the West. These rumors were definitely making their rounds, but very few of them could be confirmed. It's known that Nikolai Sokolov reportedly kept a box with many of the Romanovs' possessions, including some pearls and diamonds. Sokolov died in France in 1924, and the box and its content were later sent back to Russia.

As such, it was likely that some royalists and members of the extended royal family had access to the jewels and could have taken them out of the country. There were also early Soviet reports that described how supposedly die-hard communists were caught trying to smuggle some of the jewels out of the country. I guess the lure of easy riches was enough for some communists to drop the whole "workers of the world" routine.

Now let's look at what we definitely know:

A collection of Russian royal jewels was sold at the Christie Manson and Woods Auction House, which is today better known as Christie's, in 1927 in 124 separate lots with the profits - minus auction fees - going to the Soviet Union government.

It was believed that this was the largest portion of the royal jewels, but when a 1922 Russian language book titled *The Russian Diamond Fund* was discovered in the U.S. Geological Survey Library in Reston, Virginia, it added a new wrinkle to this mystery. According to this book, four particular gem pieces were listed that were not listed in a 1925 catalogue. One of those pieces, Empress Alexandra's crown, was sold at the 1927 Christie's auction, but the other three are still unaccounted for.

Recently, more evidence has come to light that indicates even more Romanov jewels may be floating around different locations in the world.

On August 28, 2009, the Swedish Ministry for Foreign Affairs discovered a collection of over 60 jewel-encrusted cigarette cases and cufflinks that were once owned by the Grand Duchess Vladimir (the Duchess Marie of Mecklenburg-Schwerin). Apparently, once things started going south for the Romanovs in Russia, Marie turned the jewels - which are estimated to be worth $2.6 million today - over to the Swedish embassy for safe keeping. They then ended up in the archives of the Ministry for Foreign Affairs where they were forgotten, just as the Ark of the Covenant was in *Raiders of the Lost Ark*.

Today, a large portion of the official Russian Royal jewels are kept at the Kremlin Armory Museum in Moscow, but who knows where the missing pieces are, or where the countless other pieces of "common" Romanov jewelry ended up? If some million-dollar cigarette cases were held in a warehouse for decades, there's no telling what Russian jewels are just sitting unnoticed in the private collections of wealthy people around the world.

There's a good chance that much of the missing jewelry is in the possession of people who don't know how valuable it even is! Who knows, maybe you can help solve part of this unexplained mystery by looking through some boxes in your grandparents' attic or basement!

LUCIFER BLAZED A PATH ACROSS THE BRITISH COUNTRYSIDE IN 1855

In early February 1855, the residents of South and East Devon, England were greeted with unusually heavy snowfall. Although snow is not necessarily rare in this part of southwestern England, heavy amounts are, so the local children enjoyed the rare treat.

But the treat didn't last long.

On the evenings of February 8 and 9, the residents of the region were met with something that remains unexplained. At the time, many believed it believed was otherworldly and demonic. Farmers and townspeople alike noticed that, in the freshly fallen snow, were a series of bizarre "animal" trails.

The prints resembled a single hoof print that was four inches long and three inches wide. Each print was eight to 16 inches apart in single file. As foreign as the "hoof" prints looked, their manner of movement and range was even stranger.

The hoof prints didn't seem to have any established pattern. Although the Exe Estuary was the focal point of the activity, prints were discovered over an area of 40 to 100 miles. And there were later reports of the mysterious hoof prints being found in neighboring Dorset County and as far away as the midland's county of Lincolnshire.

It also appeared as though nothing could stop the creature's movement. Homes, fences, and even rivers didn't stop the tracks. Tracks were found on top of roofs, over haystacks, and even into and out of drainpipes.

It was all very frightening to the people of the area, who began to believe that they were being visited by demons from Hell, or even Lucifer himself.

Then, as the snow melted away, so too did the sightings of the mysterious tracks.

To possibly offer some credible explanations to this unexplained mystery, we have to go back to 1855 to review the documentary evidence; unfortunately, though, there is very little. An eyewitness report in a May 1855 issue of the Australian newspaper, *Bell's Life in Sydney* described how the prints moved over walls and resembled a "donkey's shoe."

That account was the only piece of primary source evidence until a collection of personal papers belonging to the Reverend H.T. Ellacombe, the vicar of Clyst St. George, was discovered in the 1950s. The evidence included a letter from Ellacombe to another vicar discussing the incident along with drawings of the hoof prints. Because photography was still a relatively new and expensive technology in 1855, there are no photographs of the footprints.

There are a number of possible explanations for the mysterious hoofprints that were found across the English countryside in 1855. One - and I'm sure you've already thought of this - is that the sightings were a hoax.

This is often the standard or default position skeptics take on the unexplained phenomenon, but there were just too many witnesses spread out over too wide an area for it to be a coordinated hoax.

One seemingly logical explanation was that the "tracks" were made by the mooring shackles of an experimental balloon. But as credible as this explanation may sound, there are no known reports of such a balloon in the area at the time. The explanation also doesn't explain the zig-zagging movement of the prints or why the balloon wasn't caught in a tree or building and found.

The fact that the prints went in and out of four-inch diameter drainpipes has led some to suggest that hopping mice made the marks.

Other animals that have been suggested as potentially leaving the prints include badgers and even kangaroos that had escaped from a local collection. A local reverend later said he fabricated the kangaroo story to alleviate the fears of his congregation, who thought they were under a literal siege by the devil.

Although mice and/or other animals is probably the most likely explanation, there's still quite a bit that can't be explained. Mice can crawl up walls and onto rooftops, but they rarely travel in a single, straight-line when they do so. Mice also aren't known to travel to the edge of a river and stop, or possibly swim through it, and then begin their trek on the other side, as some of these prints did.

The fact that these mysterious tracks were never seen again in the area, even after significant snowfalls, also seems to be a strike against local animals being the culprit.

I guess that leaves the possibility of visitors from another world open, right?

THE MYSTERY OF THE GEORGIA GUIDESTONES

Atlanta, Georgia is a great American city with plenty of things to do. The city has great nightlife, excellent restaurants, and some beautiful parks, but if you're ever there and want to see something different, consider making a drive to rural Elbert County, 90 miles to the east.

And believe me when I say it's something different!

In a bucolic field in the middle of the county, you'll find five 16-foot-tall granite monoliths that form an "X": one slab is in the center with the other four positioned around it to form the "X." A capstone is on top of the stones to make the entire monument 19 feet, three inches tall and weighing 237,746 pounds.

The fact that a monument this size is located in the middle of nowhere is strange enough, but the mystery of the people behind the monument, and the messages inscribed on it, makes it one of the most bizarre unexplained mysteries of the modern world.

The mystery of the Georgia Guidestones, as they've become known, began in 1979 when a man using the alias "R.C. Christian" approached the owners of Elberton Granite Finishing

Company with the idea of building a strange monument on a nearby five-acre plot of land he and a group he represented had purchased. Joe Fendley, who was president of Elberton Granite at the time, gave Christian an outrageous quote.

When Christian agreed, Fendley was surprised but obligated to carry out the work. And he soon learned that it would be a job like none other.

Christian gave Fendley a ten-page book of specifications, which made the monument function as a compass, calendar, and clock. The stones were also astronomically aligned.

But the most mysterious part of the monument are the texts written on the stones, and the text on a nearby tablet that gives more details about the monument texts yet offer little that can solve the stones' mysteries.

After months of work, Elberton Granite installed the finished project and on March 22, 1980, Christian and some of his partners unveiled the cryptic monument to the world. Christian later turned ownership of the monument over to Elberton County.

Thanks to the internet, interest in the Georgia Guidestones has increased in recent years and there's been no shortage of amateur sleuths who have tried to solve its mysteries.

Other than the identity of the mysterious minds behind the monument, the most enigmatic aspect of the Georgia Guidestones is the texts.

Each face of the four stones that make the "X" have inscriptions on each side in different languages. If you read the stones clockwise from the north, they are in the following languages: English, Spanish, Swahili, Hindi, Hebrew, Arabic, Chinese, and Russian.

So far, nothing too strange. These are, after all, some of the most widely spoken languages in the world.

Each of the stones contains the ten guidelines of Christian and his group, which is where things start to get mysterious, and a bit creepy.

Most of the ten guidelines seem fair and logical, such as number five, "Protect people and nations with fair laws and just courts." Or number eight, "Balance personal rights with social duties."

But number one on the list has understandably caused plenty of controversy: "Maintain humanity under 500,000,000 in perpetual balance with nature."

Yes, you read that correctly; it's 500 *million*. And in case you're not good with numbers (they aren't my thing either, so I can definitely sympathize), the current population of the Earth is nearly eight *billion* and in 1980 it was about 4.5 *billion*. In other words, there's a pretty big discrepancy.

So, do we have any idea of who was behind the Georgia Guidestones? If we knew that, it could help us unravel the mystery of the texts.

Novelist Brad Meltzer offered a down-to-earth answer for the Guidestones, specifically the 500 million number. He said that since the monument was built during the Cold War, it was meant as a message to the survivors of a nuclear holocaust to keep the future population below that number.

Maybe, but that doesn't answer who was behind the monument's construction.

That mystery has been covered by several notable conspiracy theorists, including Jay Weidner and Alex Jones. Weidner believes that R.C. Christian was code for Christian "Rose Cross" Rosenkreuz, the legendary father of the secret Rosicrucian Order who lived in the late 14th century and early 15th centuries, although some legends state he lived even longer.

Alex Jones agrees with Weidner's assessment but added quite a few details in a 2020 documentary he filmed partially on location at the Guidestones. Jones believes that the Guidestones predict a massive culling of the world's population that has been in the works for more than 100 years. He also accused Ted Turner, the founder of the Cable News Network (CNN), of being R.C. Christian.

There's obviously no way to prove any of these conspiracy theories and the longer the Georgia Guidestones remain, the stranger they will likely get. With that said, the founders of the Georgia Guidestones and their meaning remain one of the world's strangest unexplained mysteries.

WHAT HAPPENED TO MALAYSIAN AIRLINES FLIGHT 370?

On March 8, 2014, Malaysia Airlines Flight 370 (MH370) left Kuala Lumpur International Airport in Kuala Lumpur, Malaysia for a routine flight to Beijing, China - although, it turned out, there was nothing routine about this flight. The flight began quite normally, with the crew communicating to air traffic control intermittently for about 38 minutes after takeoff, but then everything went silent.

And then things became really strange, with MH370 flying straight into becoming one of the world's unexplained mysteries.

Air traffic control screens lost MH370 minutes after the crew made their last contact, but surprisingly military radar tracked the flight for an hour as it deviated from its original flight path by traveling across the Malay Peninsula and the Andaman Sea before leaving radar range and disappearing forever.

All 12 crew members and 227 passengers were declared dead but very little evidence of the crash has ever been found, fueling conspiracy theories, and making this one of the strangest mysteries in recent years.

Extensive searches for survivors were immediately conducted by several governments but that quickly turned to a search for remains, of the plane and/or its occupants, as well as the plane's "black box," which may have yielded some answers to this perplexing tragedy.

But it wasn't until 2015 that a flaperon of one of the plane's wings washed ashore in the western Indian Ocean near Réunion Island. Then, in 2016, parts of the right stabilizer and right wing were discovered off the coast of Mozambique. Both of these discoveries are more than 2,500 miles away from Malaysia! Other small pieces of the plane were also found in other parts of the Indian Ocean, but the vast majority of MH370 was never seen again.

This brings us to the one and only question: What happened to MH370?

A number of explanations have been given by experts, and others, with some being more logical than others.

Due to the flight's sudden deviation, the most popular theories are that MH370 was hijacked or taken over in some way. ABC News and the *Los Angeles Times* were among the first mainstream news outlets to advance the theory that hijackers physically took control of the plane and then brought it to one of the hundreds of remote islands in the Indian Ocean with runways long enough to handle the landing.

This explanation seems unlikely, though, as no group has credibly claimed responsibility and there have been no signs, anywhere, of the crew or passengers. The theory also doesn't explain *why* hijackers would take the plane and everyone on it. If the hijackers, did it for profit, then a ransom would have been made by now, yet there have been no demands from kidnappers in the years since, or any claims made by potential kidnappers.

Along the same lines as a physical hijacking, some believe that MH370 was either electronically hijacked or the victim of a cyber-attack. Malaysian Prime Minister Mahathir Mohammad believed the software of the flight management system was electronically hijacked, while technology writer Jeff Wise stated that he thought that hackers did the deed.

Again, as plausible as these theories may be, there is no direct evidence to prove them. It also raises the question of who would have the ability to electronically or cyber hijack the flight, and why?

It's been suggested that Islamic jihadists were behind the crash, but none of those groups has claimed responsibility. Some have suggested that if hijacked, MH370 could have gone to North Korea, where it realistically could disappear completely given the isolation of that nation.

But as much as that would be possible, it doesn't seem very probable.

An accidental shootdown is also another possibility. These are actually a lot more common than you may think, especially when airliners are flying over or near warzones. On July 17, just over four months after MH370 disappeared, Malaysia Airlines Flight 17 was shot down over eastern Ukraine by pro-Russian rebels, killing all 283 passengers and 15 crew on the flight. So, it's not out of the realm of possibility, but again, there's no evidence that suggests this is what happened to MH370.

Other possible explanations advanced by experts include a fire or the crew becoming disorientated and flying vertically into the ocean.

With the mystery still unanswered, many conspiracy theories have surfaced. Some of the more interesting ones focused on *who* was on the plane.

One theory is that the plane was taken down to kill four inventors who were passengers on MH370. The inventors supposedly worked for Freescale Semiconductor and once they died the rights to the patent of an invention that they worked on reverted to the company. This sounds interesting, and passenger airlines have been taken down to kill fewer people (Pablo Escobar, anyone?), but there's no evidence the inventors were even on the flight.

One conspiracy theory states that MH370 was seized to obtain stealth technology from Freescale employees on the flight, while another suggests that the US took control of the plane and landed it in Diego Garcia for unspecified security reasons.

The fact that Freescale Semiconductor plays a role in two of these conspiracy theories is certainly interesting, but that's not enough alone to solve this mystery.

There are also other theories that although strange, are not totally unbelievable.

Despite you or I having a better chance of being struck by lightning, there is a chance that a meteor may have brought MH370 down. And there's also the possibility that the pilot or the entire crew decided to commit a mass murder-suicide.

For example, on October 31, 1999, EgyptAir Flight 990 was intentionally flown into the ocean by its pilot, killing all 217 passengers and crew on board, so it's not out of the realm of possibility that the crew of MH370 did the same.

And of course, how could I forget aliens and portals to other dimensions?

CNN anchor Don Lemon seriously pondered if MH370 had been sucked in by a "black hole." Maybe Lemon was playing to his audience a bit, though, as a CNN poll on its website reported that 9% of the respondents believed that MH370 was abducted by aliens, time travelers, or beings from another dimension.

Honestly, at this point, alien abduction may be as logical of an answer as any other. Many have argued that a Boeing 777 jet, which MH370 was, would have left much more debris behind if it directly hit the ocean.

So, who knows? Maybe it was aliens or maybe the passengers and crew of MH370 became part of a real-life version of *Lost*.

VICTORIAN ERA UFOS

Today, UFO sightings seem fairly commonplace thanks in part to modern technology. Cameras, home video recorders, and more recently, cellphones have all captured footage of strange objects flying in our skies that cannot be explained. Of course, many believe that these sightings are proof of alien life, while others argue they are only proof that our government, and/or corporations, have technology that is far beyond what we are commonly told. Whatever the explanation for these unexplained mysteries, you probably think that they are a fairly modern phenomena that have only been recorded for about the last 70 years, right?

Well, that's not completely true.

We aren't going to dive into an episode of *Ancient Aliens* for our next unexplained mystery, but we are going to take a look at three very strange incidents that happened over the skies of Victorian England. According to an article titled, "An Extraordinary Phenomenon," in the December 1867 issue of *Symon's Monthly Meteorological Magazine*, the people of three southeastern England communities were shocked and awed by some bizarre occurrences back then.

The first incident was reported on October 14, 1867, in Margate, County Kent. In this incident, the resident reported what sounded like a "signal gun," which was followed by thunder.

Okay, nothing too strange about this incident, but when you consider it along with the next two incidents, it appears to have been the first in a series of unexplained incidents.

On October 18, 1867, the residents of the village Thames Ditton, County Surrey, which abuts Kent's northwest border, were mystified by a strange shower from the skies. The shower lasted about ten minutes, giving witnesses quite a show as it appeared like a "shower of fire." Residents were surprised to find the next day that puddles of water in the village were covered with a layer of sulfur.

Finally, about three weeks later on November 4, southeastern England was visited once more by strange things from above. The scene of this final, and most dramatic, sighting was outside the town of Chatham in County Kent.

It took place during the afternoon between three and four p.m. According to a witness who wrote a letter to the editor of the *Chatham News*, there were "numberless black discs in groups" that were "were passing rapidly through the air."

The witness also reported that they "appeared like a large cannon shot" and that after flying around for 20 minutes they suddenly left, leaving behind a cloud of smoke.

As with the strange footprints reported across southwestern England in 1855, these bizarre incidents over the skies of southeastern were not captured on camera. Still, due to the large number of witnesses who claimed to have seen the phenomena, it's almost certain they saw *something*.

Possible explanations for the first two incidents could be rare meteorological phenomena, while the third incident could have been early hot air balloons...maybe?

The truth is you can almost certainly write off a hoax as a possible explanation. The idea of close encounters of any kind wasn't known yet to the people of the 1800s. Science fiction was a literary genre that was only beginning to become popular, so it's difficult to believe that hundreds of people in three different locations would have, or could have, conspired to create an elaborate UFO hoax. In fact, "UFO" wasn't even a term in 1867.

That leaves us with few explanations for these mysterious sightings over Victorian-era England. Weird, huh!

HOUSKA CASTLE AND THE GATEWAY TO HELL

Humans have long wondered and philosophized about the idea of God and what, if anything, comes after death. We don't know for sure, but our distant Paleolithic ancestors probably first began thinking about these things as they warmed themselves around fires in their caves after a hard day's hunt. As time went on and different human societies developed writing, questions and ideas about God and the afterlife became more detailed and developed.

Eventually, these ideas became a major part of the art of our ancestors.

Most of the art and literature about the afterlife concerns the more positive side of things, you could say. However, you don't need to look far to find some pretty scary stuff as well. For example, Dante's *Inferno* is a classic 14th-century interpretation of what Hell is like. Around that same time, a number of Renaissance artists gave their visual representations of Hell, which were often filled with awful demons and other monsters.

Today, in our modern, enlightened world we look at those paintings and stories as fiction, but what if they are all based on something real?

And if there's one place in the world that may be a portal to Hell, it is Houska Castle in the Czech Republic. Located 29 miles north of Prague, Houska Castle is very non-descript looking as far as castles are concerned, but many believe there are numerous unsolved mysteries inside its walls.

Houska Castle was built during the reign of Ottokar II, King of Bohemia (ruled 1253-1278), supposedly as an administrative center for the crown, but a close examination of castle's architecture and location reveals unexpected features.

The castle itself isn't very large and the first thing many people notice is that it doesn't have a moat or even a wall like other castles of the era. It also doesn't have a cistern for collecting drinking water and there is no kitchen, which I guess would explain why no one lived there immediately after it was completed.

Houska Castle isn't located near any trade routes, and it wasn't in a strategic location at the time. In fact, the castle was built in the middle of swamps and forests in a pretty isolated area.

As strange as all that is, the logical explanation is that it just wasn't a high-priority retreat for defense *or* relaxation. Maybe the castle was just an afterthought?

The main feature of the castle's interior is a Gothic chapel, which many believe explains the mystery of this location.

According to legends, the chapel, and the castle itself, was built on top of a hole that went all the way to Hell. The hole allowed demons and animal-human hybrids to ascend from the bowls of Hell, just like you'd see on a Renaissance painting. So, the local nobles decided to build a castle on top of it to keep the invaders in - instead of keeping them out, as is the case with all other castles.

The legend further states that before the hole was covered, local men who were condemned to death were offered pardons if they would agree to be lowered into the pit by a rope. When the first man was lowered, he almost immediately began screaming, and when they brought him back to the surface, he looked as though he had aged 30 years.

I know you're thinking, "Those are just scary stories."

But the stories just get scarier!

Another legend is that the Nazis conducted bizarre occult rituals at the castle during World War II, conjuring even more demons in the process.

Today, the mystery of the Houska Castle continues to intrigue curious people who travel there every day to see if they can solve its mysteries. Witnesses have reported hearing screams and cries at night, especially in the chapel, which appears to be the hotspot of paranormal activity.

The castle's courtyard also seems to be a vector for the undead, with numerous visitors claiming to have seen a headless entity, sometimes spouting blood from its neck as it floats around the castle...

There seems to be no rational or logical explanation for the strange occurrences at Houska Castle. A skeptical explanation may be that the awful legend of Houska Castle has had such an impact on people's imaginations that they really believe they are seeing and hearing these horrors.

Then there are those who are just playing along for the fun. It's likely that many of the "sightings" of paranormal activity at Houska Castle were from individuals who made up stories just to be part of the legend.

But no one can deny, or explain many of the seemingly supernatural incidents that have taken place at Houska Castle, or its creepy history. It's all ensured that Houska Castle has been a mystery for nearly 800 years, and it appears that it will continue to be so for another 800.

IS THERE SUCH A THING AS OCTOPUS MASS HYSTERIA?

Earlier in this book, when we examined the *Zuiyō-maru* carcass, we emphasized the vastness of the depth of the ocean. In that chapter, we considered the possibility that a strange, possibly prehistoric creature could be swimming in the depths and that the oceans still may hold many secrets and unexplained mysteries.

Another mystery of the deep took place more recently on October 27, 2017, on the seashore of County Ceredigion, Wales, United Kingdom.

On that Friday evening and throughout the rest of the weekend, residents of the largely rural county were perplexed and a little off-put to find 20 to 25 small octopuses crawling their way across New Quay Beach.

Yes, you read the correctly: A group of octopuses were *walking* along the shore.

Well, more like crawling, but the creepy sight really did happen and to this day, there are only theories to explain this otherwise baffling mystery.

The species of octopus that came to shore that weekend were curled octopuses, which are native to the waters off the British Isles and are only about the size of a human hand. Curled octopuses spend most of their lives in deep waters up to about 1,600 feet deep, so it was definitely strange to see this group on shore.

Although octopuses have been witnessed coming to shore and "walking" in other parts of the world, it's extremely rare and was unheard of in Wales - at least, up until 2017.

Local residents, fishermen, and tour guides, who are all quite familiar with the sea near New Quay Beach, told reporters this was a true anomaly. Brett Stones, who runs a local dolphin-watching guide service called SeaMôr, said: "he had never seen anything like it".

Marine biologists and other experts echoed Stone's bewilderment.

James Wright, the curator of the National Marine Aquarium in Plymouth, UK told the *Telegraph* in an interview that in addition to being a deep-sea creature, the curled octopus is "territorial and solitary," making it quite odd to see so many on a beach at the same time.

Mandy Reid, an octopus expert at the Australian Museum agreed, adding that, "Occasionally octopuses might be living in a rock pool and walk across to another rock pool to feed," but that, "Having a whole lot of them coming out onto the beach is very strange."

Very strange indeed.

There has been no lack of attempts to logically explain this inexplicable marine mystery. Wright believes there's a good chance the octopuses were washed ashore after a particularly harsh storm season. Hurricane Ophelia swept through the British Isles in early to mid-October 2017, which was followed by a storm that meteorologists named Brian, so that would appear to fit this hypothesis.

Sarah Gibbens of *National Geographic* argued that overpopulation, overfishing, and competition for food may have played a role in anomalous migration.

Other potential natural explanations include the effects of climate change, but the truth is the experts are basically at a loss, which means we get to consider other options.

Jones noted that the event was like an "end of days scenario," which has interested some who like to look beyond science for answers. The incident at New Quay Beach does sound like something you'd read in an apocalyptic text or see in a movie about the end of the world, so one wonders if some greater force was at work. Perhaps it's a sign or a warning from someone, or something, for humans to change how they treat the oceans.

Or maybe it was just octopus mass hysteria!

ALARIC'S GOLDEN TOMB

By the 5th century CE, the once-mighty Roman Empire was on its last legs, a shadow of its former self. It had been suffering from centuries of internal turmoil and decay that was at least partially the result of weak rulers and mismanagement, among a whole host of problems, about which volumes have been written.

And then there were the barbarians at the gates.

To Rome's north, west, and east, a number of primarily Germanic tribes with cool sounding names - such as the Vandals, Franks, Lombards, and Huns, just to name a few - were plundering and pillaging Roman territory and threatening Rome itself. Rome was eventually divided into two sections, East and West, with the Eastern capital based in Constantinople.

The eastern Roman Empire survived and even thrived, becoming the Byzantine Empire of the Middle Ages, but the Western Roman Empire officially ended in CE 476. Before that time, though, things got so bad that the emperor even moved his residence from Rome to the more defensible city of Ravenna, Italy.

As the Western Roman Empire was collapsing, a man named Alaric (ruled CE 395-410), who was the king of the Germanic tribe known as the Visigoths, made a bold play for power and wealth that resulted in his death but also gave birth to an unexplained mystery.

When Alaric became king of the Visigoths, he had a vision unlike most of his predecessors. He wasn't content with just plundering and pillaging, or even fighting as mercenaries *for* Rome, as many Germanic tribes of the time did. No, he wanted his people to have a permanent place to call their own within Roman territory with the full benefits of being Roman citizens.

The Romans weren't too keen on Alaric's idea, so war broke out, but the virile Visigoths were able to overcome the weakened Romans. Alaric led his people to the gates of Rome in 408 and laid siege to the city. The soft Romans weren't ready for a long siege, so the Roman Senate agreed to pay off Alaric to leave. They gave him 5,000 pounds of gold, 30,000 pounds of silver, 4,000 silk tunics, 3,000 scarlet hides, and 3,000 pounds of pepper. The gold alone would be worth over one hundred and thirty million dollars in today's market.

It was definitely a nice haul, but Alaric wanted more. He wanted the Western Emperor Honorius to make him head of the Roman Army and he still wanted land for his people, although that wasn't one of his initial demands. On the other hand, Honorius was looking for any opportunity he could to rid Italy of the Visigoths and to avoid giving Alaric what he wanted.

Things finally came to a head in 409 when Roman troops attacked some of Alaric's men who were marching to Ravenna, leading to a second Visigoth siege of Rome that year. It was during this siege that Alaric demanded land for himself and his people in the Roman province of Noricum.

But the emperor wasn't playing along.

Finally, on August 24, 410, Alaric was done playing games with the Romans. He unleashed his army, which numbered as many as 40,000, on the citizens of the all-but-undefended Rome. The Visigoths raped and pillaged the city and its citizens for three days, only leaving the churches untouched.

When the Visigoths' orgy of violence had finally ended, they took just about everything of value that they could move, including slaves, and marched south.

The ancient and early medieval historical sources state that Alaric planned to cross from the Italian Peninsula to Sicily and then sail from Sicily to North Africa where they would cut off Rome's grain supply.

But in war things often don't go as planned, and here's where our mystery becomes more interesting.

In 411, the Visigoths were in the southern Italian region of Bruttium (modern Calabria) when Alaric died near the city of Consentia (modern Cosenza). The cause of Alaric's death is itself a mystery. While many modern scholars believe it was the result of illness (perhaps Malaria), others think it may have been caused by an infection from a battle wound. Others still think he was murdered!

All of those would have been common ways for an ancient Germanic warlord to die.

The true mystery begins *after* Alaric died and concerns all those treasures that he took from Rome in 408 and 410. According to the legends, Alaric and all his treasures were buried *underneath* the Busento River, which is a small tributary of the Crati River.

Unlike some of these other legends discussed in this book, there is actually a written document that supports this legend.

The 6th-century Byzantine-Gothic historian, Jordanes, wrote:

> *"To this place came Alaric, king of the Visigoths, with the wealth of all Italy which he had taken as spoil, and from there, as we have said, he intended to cross over by way of Sicily to the quiet land of Africa. But since man is not free to do anything he wishes without the will of God, that dread strait sunk several of his ships and threw all into confusion. Alaric was cast down by this reverse and, while deliberating what he should do, was suddenly overtaken by an untimely death and departed from human cares. His people mourned for him with the utmost affection. Then turning from this course the river Busentus near the city of Consentia - for this stream flows with its wholesome waters from the foot of a mountain near that city - they led a band of captives into the midst of its bed to dig out a place for his grave. In the depths of this pit they buried Alaric, together with many treasures, and then turned the waters back into their channel. And that none might ever know the place, they put to death all the diggers."*

It's estimated that if this golden tomb does exist, there may be up to 25 tons of gold in it, along with numerous other pieces of jewelry, statues, and other priceless artifacts equaling around one billion euros.

For centuries, people all but forgot about Alaric's Golden Tomb. Literacy was low until the modern era, so most people couldn't read Jordanes' Latin text and those who could were too busy surviving the Middle Ages and early modern era.

But the 20th century brought new levels of literacy and interest in the past from many different quarters.

British novelist George Gissing took an interest in the story after reading Edward Gibbon's The History of the Decline and Fall of the Roman Empire, even traveling to Cosenza in 1897 to possibly locate the tomb.

Interested in the potential of the gold funding their war machine, as well as esoteric reasons, the Nazis and their fascist Italian allies also took an interest in Alaric's tomb in the 1930s. Henrich Himmler, the head of the SS, was said to have searched for the tomb in 1937.

After World War II, interest in Alaric's tomb was relegated to the fringes of the archaeological and historical worlds. Then, in 2015, Italian archaeologists embarked on an extensive project that combined the use of drones, ground-penetrating radar, and infrared technology, along with Jordanes' account. The archaeologists believe they have narrowed the possibility to five sites.

Others have already stated to have located the tomb.

Merlin Burrows claimed on his 2017 website to have found the tomb and invites anyone interested to contact him. Apparently, no press conference was given.

Numerous other internet sleuths and amateur historians have also given their opinions, although as is often the case, the skeptics get the most attention. They correctly point out that the region has experienced several earthquakes in the last 1,500 years that have shifted the Busento River enough that it surely would have revealed a subterranean tomb by now.

Other skeptics note that building such an elaborate tomb would have required more sophisticated engineering than the Visigoths had access to and too many people would have known about it. Even if all of Alaric's men kept quiet, their only option to keep the townsfolk quiet would have been to massacre all of them - and there is nothing in the records about such an act.

Still, none of these objections absolutely discount the possibility.

The Busento River is relatively narrow and shallow, so diverting it wouldn't have required extensive engineering knowledge, and according to Francesco Sisci, the coordinator of the 2015 archaeological project, the tomb could be deep enough to be protected from earthquakes.

With all of that said, other theories should be considered to possibly answer this unexplained mystery.

Many modern historians believe that although Alaric was probably buried somewhere in southern Italy, it was likely in a much less ornate tomb than we might expect. They argue that the vast majority of the treasure taken from Rome was inherited by Alaric's successor, Athaulf, which he took with him to Gaul before moving on to Spain.

Although this is the most logical answer, the haul the Visigoths took in 408 and 410 was so large that one would think a hefty cache of at least part of it would have been discovered somewhere. Even a small amount of the overall haul would be significant and would be nearly impossible to hide once found. This is particularly the case since Spain became a battleground between the Romans, Visigoths, Vandals, and Alans for the next 300 years, with the Visigoths first taking control before falling to the Moors in 711.

There is not one report of any of these kingdoms, which were constantly in need of funds to pay their armies, suddenly coming into large amounts of gold or silver.

It's as if all the treasures of Rome vanished in 411. Where they are, and where Alaric was buried, remains one of history's greatest unexplained mysteries.

THE BLOODY BENDERS

Today many people look back on 19th-century frontier America with a sort of nostalgia. Although no one alive today experienced the 1800s, some of us long for those simpler times when things were truly black and white. Some yearn for the tight family unit depicted on the TV show *Little House on the Prairie*, while others wish to emulate the quick justice as depicted on shows such as *Gunsmoke*.

But the truth is things weren't always so great in the 1800s.

Yes, there were indeed fewer social problems and families were more intact, but that's partially because the family unit was all the support on offer on the American frontier. Families had to be their own police and doctors in the absence of official institutions.

And it wasn't like crime didn't exist on the frontier.

The stories you've read about outlaws as well as ones you've probably seen in TV documentaries were more or less true, although they were also usually less romantic in real life. The reality is that frontier criminals could be pretty brutal, and thanks to the lack of official law in many parts, their fates were often decided in equally brutal ways.

Many outlaws who lived by the gun died by the gun, or they were strung up at the end of a rope by angry lynch mobs.

But occasionally some of those outlaws got away with their crimes. Remember, this was long before the internet, and photography was fairly new even in the late 1800s, so some sly criminals were able to stay one step ahead of law enforcement.

This was the case of the Bender family in rural southeastern Kansas, commonly known as the "Bloody Benders," who it is said, robbed and murdered as many as 20 people from May 1871 to April 1873. Many unsolved mysteries surround this early case of American true crime history, including: Who exactly were the Benders, how many people did they kill, and most importantly, what happened to them?

The background of the Bender family is as enigmatic as their eventual disappearance. The family was headed by John Sr. (Pa), his wife Elvira (Ma), and also comprised their children, son John Jr. and daughter Kate. The Bender parents are believed to have been German immigrants, with their original family name possibly being Flickinger, although this isn't known for sure. Other reports said they were possibly Dutch, leaving the family's national/ethnic origins a question.

Ma and Pa spoke in heavy accents that were at times unintelligible to the locals, but they may have used that to their advantage.

The nature of John Jr. and Kate's relationship was also never clearly defined. Most believed they were siblings, although newspapers reported they were married, and other witnesses claimed they had an incestuous relationship.

The Benders set up their homestead in a small, two-room house on the plains outside the town of Oswego, Kansas. The Benders operated a small farm, but the core of their business, as well as their nefarious activities, took place in the house. They converted the front room into a general store and inn for weary travelers.

It was also where several men and at least one child met their demise.

It's believed that victims, who were usually weary travelers, would be given a "seat of honor" at the table that was in front of a curtain and on top of a trap door. The attractive young Kate would distract the victims with small talk, or stories about spiritualism, after which one or both of the Bender men would emerge from behind the curtain and ambush the hapless victim.

A hammer was the preferred murder weapon, but more than a dozen bullet holes were later found in the roof and walls of the cabin, suggesting some victims were shot. With the victim on the floor from the hammer blow, the Bender women would then finish the deed by cutting the throat of the incapacitated victim. The body was then dropped through the trap door to the cellar where the Benders could pilfer it for its belongings before dismembering and burying it in the yard.

Since the Benders profited very little from the robberies, it's believed by many that they simply enjoyed killing.

The Bender murders are believed to have started in May 1871, and as they progressed over the next two years, and some bodies began turning up, people in the rural county started to worry. The first identified murder was on 1 May 1871 and the last identified murder on 20 May 873.

But this was frontier America, so little was done by local law enforcement. Not that there was much of a local enforcement presence in the area anyway.

Everything came to a head when the Benders killed the wrong person.

In the winter of 1872, George Newton Longcor left nearby Independence, Kansas with his infant daughter. They were headed for Iowa but never made it to their destination. Their disappearance led to their former neighbor, William Henry York, setting out to find them, but he too disappeared.

York's brother was Colonel Alexander M. York, a Civil War veteran and current member of the Kansas State Senate. Alexander York was determined to get to the bottom of his brother's disappearance, which brought him to the Benders' home on March 28, 1873. The Benders admitted William had stayed there but blamed his disappearance on Indians. Alexander believed them for the time being and left.

It was 1800s frontier America, after all, and Indians were the equivalent of the boogeyman at the time.

York returned on April 3 but was told by Kate to come back later, alone.

When York and several men did return several weeks later with warrants to search every farm in the Osage Township, the Benders had vanished.

Colonel York and several area men searched the Bender farm, discovering several buried bodies and a plethora of body parts.

Although frontier outlaws were common in the 1800s, this type of serial murder was unheard of, so the case quickly garnered plenty of media attention and law enforcement in the state of Kansas.

In their hasty retreat, the Benders left a trail that detectives were able to follow to Denison, Texas. From there, it's believed the Benders went to a lawless region along the Texas-New Mexico border where they were able to live out the rest of their lives in relative comfort.

Or did they?

There are plenty of theories concerning the fate of the Benders, some of which are more credible than others. A detective who claimed to have continued the pursuit of the Benders said that John Junior died of apoplexy on the frontier while Pa and Elvira went north, eventually ending up in St. Louis where they disappeared.

The whereabouts of Kate was never stated in this theory.

One of the more credible Bender sightings happened in 1889 in Michigan. On October 30, 1889, two women - Almira Monroe and Sarah Eliza Davis - were arrested for larceny in Michigan but released from jail several weeks later when they were found not guilty.

By then, technology had finally caught up with the Bender's criminal ways, as witnesses from Kansas identified Monroe and Davis as Ma and Kate Bender respectively, which was then apparently confirmed by photographs. Davis told the authorities that Monroe was, in fact, Ma Bender but that she wasn't Kate. The two women were extradited to Labette County, Kansas, where the pair both claimed not to be the Benders but instead two other notorious criminals.

Many locals were convinced they were the Bender women, but the judge wasn't, so he released them. The two mysterious women were never heard from again.

There were numerous other Bender sightings throughout the US for the next several decades.

One of the most interesting leads came from Montana in 1884. According to that report, an elderly man murdered a man with a hammer in Idaho before fleeing to Montana where he was arrested. His MO, age (the killer was in his early 70s, about the same age as Pa Bender), and physical description all fit Pa Bender. But the killer cut his foot off to free himself from a leg iron and escaped the jail.

The suspect died and his body decomposed before a positive ID could be made.

Another legend states that all the Benders were shot and killed by an angry mob, except for Kate, who was burned alive!

Eventually, the people of southeastern Kansas moved on, but the mystery of the fate of the Bloody Benders was never completely forgotten, always there lurking in the background like a boogeyman.

DID THE MISSING
LINK DIE IN 2012?

When Charles Darwin's *'On the Origins of Species'* was first published in 1859, it created scientific and social shockwaves that are still reverberating throughout the world. The theory of evolution became official dogma in the scientific disciplines of biology and anthropology, and the idea that modern humans were descended from more primitive primates began to gain ground.

The bones of primitive human races were discovered, but missing from all these discoveries, at least in the minds of many, was the "missing link" species that connected humans to apes.

Then, in 1976, people around the world thought the missing link had been found!

In the spring of 1976, at the annual Explorer's Club dinner in New York City, animal trainer Frank Berger first introduced a very strange looking and acting chimpanzee named Oliver to the world. The film footage was nothing short of amazing.

The "chimp" walked upright bipedally in a gait that more closely resembled a human's than an ape. Oliver was also bald, and his head appeared smaller than the average chimp's. His jaw was far less pronounced, he had light colored eyes, and it was said that his scent was different as well.

Experts, witnesses, and those who knew Oliver described him as "strange," "different," and "more than an animal." And some even went as far to claim he was proof of the missing link between human and ape and that he must be some type of human-ape hybrid, a "humanzee."

Oliver was sent to Japan to be investigated by experts under intense media scrutiny, and although some of the mysteries of this scientific oddity were eventually answered, many questions still remain unanswered.

Oliver is believed to have been born sometime in the late 1950s in central Africa. He was brought to the United States by animal trainer Frank Berger and lived with him and his wife Janet until 1976.

It was immediately apparent to the Bergers that Oliver was unlike any of the hundreds of chimps they had previously owned. But the Bergers really knew they had something different on their hands when, according to Janet, at the age of four or five months, Oliver suddenly stood upright.

In addition to Oliver's strange appearance and upright posture, Janet Berger claims he preferred the company of humans and was generally disliked by other chimps.

Janet Berger also said that Oliver's behavior around the home was very un-ape like. He smoked cigars, would do chores such as moving hay around the property in a wheelbarrow and would wash his hands.

The Bergers sold Oliver to a New York City lawyer named Michael Miller in 1976, which began a long and often difficult life for the chimp that included several different moves and owners. But before Miller sold the exceptional primate, he arranged to have him sent to Japan for some testing.

A number of scientists gave Oliver a battery of tests, with many claiming that he was more human than ape. The major revelation was believed to have been a test that revealed he had 47 chromosomes, not the 48 that chimps have but also not the 46 of humans.

Many thought that this proved Oliver was the missing link; unfortunately for him, the attention span of modern people is short. After falling from the headlines, Oliver was passed around some different owners until he was transferred to the primate sanctuary, Primarily Primates, in 1998.

But before Oliver arrived at his new and final home, samples of his DNA were taken in 1996 for more advanced testing.

The test revealed that Oliver was, in fact, a chimp with 48 chromosomes, proving that he was not the missing link. Yet it doesn't answer all of the questions surrounding this amazing and mysterious creature.

It has never been explained how the results of Oliver's earlier chromosome test resulted in 47 chromosomes instead of 48.

Geneticist Dr. John Ely examined Oliver's DNA sequence for a 2006 Discovery Channel special, confirming that Oliver was a chimp with 48 chromosomes. With that said, Ely noted that details of Oliver's genetic markers were unique.

"Oliver is different from your common chimpanzee from West Africa," Ely said.

The slight genetic variation Ely found in Oliver's DNA may partially explain his unique appearance and temperament, but many questions remain.

Wallace Swett, the former director of Primarily Primates, noted how even after living in a small cage for nine years previously, Oliver immediately walked upright when he arrived at the Texas facility.

Other experts have claimed that Oliver's features are within the range of normal chimpanzees, but these same experts can never produce another example of a chimp that looks or acts like Oliver.

So, what are some of the possible explanations for Oliver?

Some have suggested he is some type of mutant ape, perhaps a throwback subspecies that although genetically a chimp, was a living example of how primates did, in fact, make the leap to human.

Skeptics have suggested that Oliver was simply taught to walk and act as he did from an early age, but Swett is quick to refute such claims.

"Oliver's stance when he walks is with his shoulders back and his knees locked. And there's never, ever, been a chimpanzee trained to walk that has been able to keep that pose," Swett said.

Oliver took the secrets of his appearance and behavior with him to the grave in 2012. Those who find this mystery tragic should take heart in the fact that he lived his last few years in comfort and with a female companion named Raisin, who was there when he died. Perhaps the true unexplained mystery of Oliver concerns how humans treat each other, and animals, and how that will relate to our future.

CHILDREN FROM
ANOTHER DIMENSION

Earlier in our book we took a look at a UFO sighting from the 19th century that caused quite a stir in southeastern England. More than 700 years earlier, the people of the village of Woolpit in County Suffolk in the East Anglia region of eastern England, were greeted with a different kind of close encounter that remains one of the most bizarre unexplained mysteries of the Middle Ages.

According to two medieval writers - Ralph of Coggeshall (died c. 1266) in his chronicle *Chronicum Anglicanum* and William of Newburgh (c. 1136-1198) in his work, *Historia rerum Anglicarum* - the people of this quaint English village were visited by two children who may have been from another dimension. Alternatively, they could have just had some illness that medieval medicine could neither identify nor treat.

The incident took place in the fall during the reign of King Stephen (ruled 1135-1154). The exact year is not known and it's not very important. What's important is that according to William, the people of Woolpit found a young girl and a young boy near a wolf pit. This is a bit strange to begin with, but the story only gets stranger.

Neither child could speak English, they were wearing strange clothing, and most mysterious of all, their skin was described as green in color!

The account states that, after the children were taken in by a local leader named Richard de Calne, they only ate raw broad beans at first. Once they began consuming normal food, however, their green hue eventually faded.

The children were baptized but the boy unfortunately died so whatever secrets he may have held were lost with him. The girl, though, stayed in the village and eventually learned English. According to Ralph, she related her background to the villagers, and it was nothing short of fantastic.

The girl said they came from a land known as St. Martin's Land, where everything was green and devoid of sunlight. Apparently, what little light they did get was like twilight. She went on to say that they were herding their family's cattle when some went into a cave. They followed the cattle into the cave but came out on the other side to Woolpit.

According to modern writer Duncan Lunan, the girl may have been named Agnes and she probably married a royal official named Richard Barre, although this isn't definite.

So, what are some possible explanations for the green children of Woolpit, and do they hold up to scrutiny?

Well, the first logical explanation would be that the story was simply made up and that it was a hoax. Although this would probably be the skeptic's first choice of an explanation for such an event in the modern era, it just doesn't hold up for the Middle Ages. People at that time didn't develop hoaxes - for fun or otherwise - and it should be pointed out that William and Ralph were both members of the Church.

Lying, especially in an official Church document, would be a serious violation of the Ten Commandments and Church doctrine. No, William and Ralph may not have seen the children themselves, but they were reporting the events as they were related to them.

Of course, this means they could have been given some colorfully elaborated facts.

Some modern scholars believe that the incident was a retelling of ancient British folklore. Church historians often did relate ancient pre-Christian myths in their writings, especially in ethnographies or local histories, but the context of both accounts is clearly written as recounting of facts following standard medieval historiographical style.

So, if the stories aren't hoaxes or fanciful retellings of folktales, that only leaves the possibility that this did happen, more or less.

The most logical explanation was offered by historian Paul Harris, who believes the children were lost Flemish immigrants. He points out that many Flemish immigrants arrived in that region of England just before the children were found and many lived in the village of Fornham St. Martin. This would explain the "St. Martin Land" the girl spoke about as well as the children being unable to speak English and possibly even their different clothing.

Harris further added that their green hue may have been the result of hypochromic anemia, which then cleared up when they were given a proper diet.

As plausible as this explanation is, there are some problems with it. For instance, the girl's guardian, Richard de Calne, was educated and likely would have recognized Flemish, if that's what they spoke, as a European language. Also, the girl's description of St. Martin's Land does not match anything in this world.

So, that brings us to the other worldly explanations.

The idea that the green children were from another planet or dimension was first suggested in the 17th century when Robert Burton wrote in *The Anatomy of Melancholy* that the children "fell from Heaven."

In 1996, astronomer Duncan Lunan offered a much more detailed thesis regarding the children's extraterrestrial origins. He wrote that the children were transported to Woolpit accidentally and that their color was the result of a diet of genetically modified plants on their home planet.

It isn't clear how Lunan learned these details but at this point, until more green children are found wandering the countryside, it's as good as any other explanation for this mystery.

KING SOLOMON'S MINES

Our next unexplained mystery involves a search for a legendary treasure that has spanned centuries, utilizing archaeological and historical methods of research in the process. The quest is for the legendary mines of King Solomon, and perhaps what makes this such a great unexplained mystery is how difficult it is to cut through all the fiction surrounding it.

And there's plenty of it!

The best place to begin this mystery is with the historical King Solomon before moving forward to examine some of the theories and attempts to find this great treasure cache.

King Solomon *(ruled c. 1002-962 BCE; other sources list his rule as c. 970-931 BCE but reliable dating is not available)* was the king of the ancient Kingdom of Israel, having inherited the throne from his father, David. Solomon was lauded in the biblical books of Kings and Chronicles for his wisdom and intelligence, but also his wealth.

It's Solomon's wealth and where he kept it hidden that's our interest.

According to the Christian Old Testament book 1 Kings, Solomon received cargo shipments from a mysterious and as yet unidentified land named Ophir every three years.

1 Kings 10:22-23 states: "For the king had at sea a navy of Tharshish with the navy of Hiram: once in three years came the navy of Tharshish, bringing gold, and silver, ivory, and apes, and peacocks. So King Solomon exceeded all the kings of the earth for riches and wisdom."

Searches and theories about the location of Solomon's treasures, which became known in popular legend's as "Solomon's mines," were also connected to his relationship with the legendary Queen of Sheba. Solomon was quite the ladies' man, amassing many wives and concubines in addition to plenty of gold and other commodities. According to the Bible, when Sheba visited him, she added to that wealth.

1 Kings 10:2: "And she came to Jerusalem with a very great train, with camels that bare spices, and very much gold, and precious stones: and when she was come to Solomon, she communed with him all that was in her heart."

In subsequent centuries, the ideas of Solomon's lost wealth took on a life of its own, with modern interest being firmly traced to Englishman H. Rider Haggard's 1885 novel, *King Solomon's Mines*. Although Haggard's novel was pure fiction and placed the legendary mines in sub-Saharan Africa, it renewed interest in the mystery. Four film and miniseries versions of the novel have been produced, and countless people around the world have attempted to find the mines, some taking a more scientific tack than others.

The more scientific approach to solving this mystery began with mid-20th century American archaeologist Nelson Glueck. By comparing the biblical accounts with archaeological evidence that he uncovered in southern Israel, Glueck argued that Solomon's mines were located in the Great Rift Valley just south of the Dead Sea in what was the ancient land of Edom.

Glueck argued that Solomon's mines in Edom were rich in copper and iron, which in terms of early Iron Age warfare and tools were probably more important for Solomon than gold or silver.

In 2008, Israeli archaeologists located other potential ancient mining sights in modern-day Jordan that may have been a mining site during Solomon's reign, but the most intriguing prospect was located a few years later in Israel's Timna Valley. The site shows signs of ancient copper-smelting activity, but scholars are unsure if it is old enough to have been used during Solomon's rule.

This all sounds reasonable, but it really doesn't solve the mystery of where all the gold and other goodies mentioned in the biblical passages earlier came from, or where they went. The archaeological work done by Glueck and others proves that Solomon may have had copper and iron mines in southern Israel, but the location or even the existence of Ophir remain a mystery.

Throughout the centuries since the Bible was put into writing, many scholars and adventurers have equated Ophir with the lost mines of Solomon. The Alexandrian geographer Ptolemy (c. CE 100-170) theorized that Ophir was located at the mouth of the Indus River, in what is today Pakistan.

Later European and early Islamic scholars also placed Ophir in India as well as Sri Lanka, the Philippines, and sub-Saharan Africa.

Today, searches for Ophir have been relegated to the background of the more scientific excavations in Israel and Jordan, but there are those who still believe that the location of the mysterious place, and King Solomon's wealth, is waiting to be found by a soul as adventuresome as Allan Quatermain, the hero of Haggard's novel.

THE SOLWAY
FIRTH SPACEMAN

On May 23, 1964, firefighter Jim Templeton and his wife Annie decided to take their 5-year-old daughter Elizabeth on a short get-away from their Carlisle, England home. They went a few miles north to the village of Burgh Marsh, which is on the border of Scotland and England, to a quiet location that overlooks the Solway Firth.

The weather was cool and breezy, yet sunny; everything they would expect on a late spring day in northwestern England. So, Jim took some pictures of his wife and daughter and then they went home.

When the Templetons received their photos back a few days later (you had to actually go to a lab to get your pictures developed back then!) they were shocked by what they found in one of the photos.

There sat Elizabeth, smiling for the camera, but beyond her several feet was a figure apparently looking over the firth. The more Jim and Annie looked at the photo, the more creeped out they became. The build of the figure indicated it was a fit male, but the strangest part was what he - or it - was wearing.

The figure appeared to be dressed in an all-white uniform of some type and what seemed to be a helmet. The mysterious figure looked like an astronaut or something from outer space!

Stories like this have a way of traveling quickly in small towns, and before too long the local newspaper, *The Cumberland News*, ran a story on the incident. National publications such as *The Daily Mail* and *Express* then ran the story, with the photo of what became known as the "Solway Firth Spaceman."

Although this was long before photoshop and digital cameras, which can allow a person to create some out-of-this-world images, hoxes were possible and did happen. They usually involved paper plates and wires to create flying saucers/UFOs, but since this one involved what looked like a person, it was a bit different from your garden variety UFO picture. Kodak, the company that developed the film, examined the photo and determined that it was real.

Or, at least, there really was a figure standing behind Elizabeth. Kodak could not determine who or what it was.

According to Jim Templeton, the media frenzy over his photo brought him some unwanted attention. He said that not long after the photo was published, he was visited by two men who claimed to work for the British government and "that they were only identified by number." They brought him to the location of the sighting, but when Templeton told the men he never actually saw the figure, they angrily left him stranded at the firth.

This "men in black" encounter certainly adds another layer of mystery to this already mysterious story, but it should be pointed out that Templeton thought the two men were pulling a prank on him and weren't actual government agents.

Still, that leaves this strange photo that Kodak insisted wasn't doctored. So, what are some possible explanations?

Everyone who has studied this case thinks that the Templetons believe they saw something. There's nothing to suggest either of the parents *knowingly* posed for the shot or that they had someone else pose. There's also little information to suggest that it was an accidental photo bomb. The Templetons said the only other people they saw at the firth that day were two older ladies, and the figure in the photo doesn't look like a woman.

UFO expert Dr. David Clarke believed there is a reasonable explanation for the photo, however.

"One of the other stills [taken that day] shows Jim's wife who, according to him, was standing behind him when he took the photo of Elizabeth," Clarke said. "I think for some reason his wife walked into the shot and he didn't see her because with that particular make of camera you could only see 70% of what was in the shot through the viewfinder."

That certainly sounds logical, but I just can't get over how the mystery figure looks like a male. You can see that the arms and back are quite muscular, with the latissimus dorsi muscles (lats) being even wider than that of the average man.

As people looked for terrestrial explanations for the Solway Firth Spacemen, some pointed toward a nearby Air Force installation. The British RAF Spadeadam station was located just a few miles to the west of the Solway Firth Spaceman sighting and although most of what was taking place there was top secret in 1964, it was later revealed to be the place where Britain assembled their Blue Streak missiles.

This is certainly interesting, especially because UFO sightings are more common around military bases, but there are a couple of problems with this theory. First, the British RAF claims all of the missiles were tested in Australia and later in South America. Even if the RAF was conducting secret missile tests in the area, it doesn't explain the appearance of the figure in Jim Templeton's photo.

So that leaves us with otherworldly explanations.

County Cumbria has traditionally been one of the top locations for UFO sightings in the United Kingdom, although that may have to do with military bases in the region. Skeptics have also pointed out that if aliens were visiting our planet, why would they dress like human astronauts as the Solway Firth Spaceman apparently did.

That leaves us with more mystical explanations.

As UFO lore has become less cool in the 2010s and beyond, it's been replaced with ghost hunting and interest in paranormal activity. Some fans of the Solway Firth Spaceman incident have argued that it was indeed from another world, but that it was the world of the undead.

Technological advances in photography may help solve the mystery of the Solway Firth Spaceman, but for now, your guess is as good as any other concerning its origin.

LISTEN FOR THE HUMMING THE NEXT TIME YOU'RE IN TAOS

Taos, New Mexico is a sleepy little town in the northcentral part of the state that's known for its friendliness, southwestern architecture, and some excellent skiing. Yep, Taos is a pretty quiet town, for the most part.

But if you're one of the approximately 2% of the population who can hear the "Taos Hum," then the artsy little town may not seem so quiet.

For quite some time, although it isn't known for sure how long, many residents of Taos have reported hearing a constant, low volume hum. As news of this phenomenon spread during the late 1980s, University of New Mexico professors Joe Mullins and Jim Kelly decided to investigate things further. They conducted a series of tests on area residents who claimed to hear the hum and published their findings on November 22, 1995.

A number of devices were installed in the homes of the lucky 2% who claimed to hear the buzzing, but the tests didn't reveal anything special about the environment. With that said, the interviews of the "hearers" did uncover something notable that only seemed to deepen this mystery.

The respondents claimed to hear different sounds. For some, it was a buzz, while for others it was a whir. The only thing that the hearers seemed to agree on was that the sound was constant yet barely audible.

The research left Mullins and Kelly with no true explanation for the mystery, but they had their own theories and plenty of other people have come up with their own ideas.

One logical explanation is that the hearers of the hum are suffering from a form of tinnitus. Tinnitus is the term for any type of "ringing" sound a person hears without there being an external stimulus for that sound. Tinnitus can be caused by several different things, and partly because of that, it is not completely understood by experts.

Tinnitus may explain some cases of the Taos buzzing, but not all, especially those where beats are reported along with the buzzing since beats do not accompany tinnitus cases.

Another potential medical explanation for this mystery is a phenomenon known as spontaneous otoacoustic emission (SOAE). That's a mouthful - or an earful, in this case - but it simply refers to sounds generated in the inner ear without external stimuli. The difference between SOAE and tinnitus is that with SOAE actual measurable sounds are being created.

As with tinnitus, SOAE could account for some of the Taos buzzing cases, but not all of them.

So, what are we left with for explanations?

Some have suggested that the buzzing is the result of a combination of airplanes, other industrial noises, and hoaxes.

These may account for some of the reports, but there are just too many cases, and they are too persistent, to be simply written off as misheard sounds or pranks.

That leaves us with some of the more imaginative explanations. Taos is, after all, quite a unique place.

Aliens and UFOs have been a popular explanation for the Taos buzzing. New Mexico has consistently been one of the top states for UFO sightings and it was about 260 miles to the south of Taos where the greatest unexplained UFO incident took place in Roswell, New Mexico in 1947.

Another possible theory, which is sometimes linked to the UFO theory, is that the buzzing is the result of a military or CIA experiment. There are a number of military installations in the region, and the Los Alamos laboratory is a relatively short distance from Taos, so it's not out of the realm of possibility that people are hearing some type of ongoing top-secret experiment.

At this point, the origins of the buzzing are anyone's guess, but if you ever happen to be in Taos, pay real careful attention. You may be one of the 2%!

MAKE IT RAIN WELL, DON DECKER REALLY COULD!

On February 26, 1983, Don Decker was a troubled 21-year-old man from Stroudsburg, Pennsylvania who was sitting in the Monroe County Jail on a one-year felony conviction for receiving stolen property. Decker's wild, criminal lifestyle caused a rift between him and his family. By that time, he had become all but estranged from most of them.

But then his grandfather, James Kishaugh, died and the county officials agreed to give Decker a furlough for a few days to attend the funeral and visit family.

This is where a difficult yet normal story of a man with family problems veered into the unexplained.

Decker attended the funeral, but things were a little tense between him and his family. Kishaugh had physically abused Decker when he was a child, and he'd kept it secret from the family his entire life. Decker kept all those feelings pent up inside him for more than ten years and when he attended the funeral, they came flooding out in a torrent of emotions.

"No other part of the family knew anything about what happened," Decker recalled in an interview on a 1993 episode of *Unsolved Mysteries*. "The evil was gone and I was hoping, you know, that everything would change."

The evil was far from gone in Decker's life, but he was correct that everything would change.

Instead of staying with his estranged family during his furlough, Decker went to visit his friends, Bob and Jeannie Keiffer. As soon as he arrived, things started to get really weird.

When Decker entered the living room of the Keiffer's home, the room suddenly got very cold and then water began dripping from the walls. Perhaps even creepier, Don went into a trance and either couldn't or wouldn't communicate with his friends. Disturbed by the situation and not knowing what to do about the "leak," the Kieffers called their landlord, Ron Van Why.

As a landlord, Van Why was handy and had seen some strange things at his rental homes, but this was like nothing else. There were no pipes in the living room where the water was coming from and as the phenomenon continued, he noticed that it was no natural "leak."

"It could come from the wall over or from the floor up," Van Why noted about the water. "There was no basic direction that it was coming from."

Van Why then called his wife to come and witness the phenomenon, and after she saw it, they called the local police.

Local police officers Richard Wolbert and John Baujan were equally perplexed and disturbed by what they saw. And it seems that as time went on, it only got stranger.

"We were standing just inside the front door and met this droplet of water traveling horizontally. It passed between us and just traveled out into the next room," said Wolbert.

Then things went into *The Exorcist* territory.

As the event was unfolding, the Kieffers and Decker went to a nearby pizza restaurant to "cool down" while the police and the Van Whys stayed behind to find a solution for the creepy incident. Miraculously, the rain stopped inside the Keiffer home…but began at the pizza parlor!

Pam Scrofano's, the owner of the pizza parlor, claims that she took a crucifix and placed it on Decker, causing him to recoil in pain from a burning sensation.

The police chief later arrived at the Keiffer home and declared it a plumbing problem. That's it, case closed, or case covered up?

Well, the local police went behind their chief's back and returned to the Keiffer home the next day. The police knew that something was happening with Don Decker and in the small, rural, and conservative town of Stroudsburg, many began to think demonic possession was the culprit.

According to witnesses, officer Bill Davies gave Decker a crucifix, and just as on the previous night, it burned his hand. Witnesses then claimed that Decker levitated, and claw marks appeared on his neck.

The Van Whys decided to take things into their own hands by finding a preacher to do an exorcism. According to them, it was temporarily successful, as the activity in the home stopped. However, whatever it was followed Decker when he was returned to jail the next day.

The mysterious indoor rain began happening within the walls of the Monroe County Jail after a few days. Decker later claimed that at that point he could make his cell "rain" by concentrating hard enough, which was enough to get the attention of the very religious warden, David Keenhold.

As with the many witnesses who saw Decker make it rain days earlier, Keenhold was convinced the inmate was possessed by demons, so he wasted no time bringing in Reverend William Blackburn to take charge of the case.

Blackburn was actually skeptical, to begin with, but after meeting Decker, his attitude changed.

Blackburn said that when he met Decker, the room they were in smelled like death and that he challenged Decker on his claim to make it rain at will.

"He raised his hand and rubbed his fingers together. And all of a sudden, it started to rain," Blackburn said.

Blackburn then said that he prayed for Decker and the rain finally stopped.

Decker later said that the rain never happened again, but after 1993, he all but dropped out of the public eye. His case grabbed media attention briefly again in 2012 when he was arrested in an arson case, but his apparent ability to make it rain, had no role in the alleged crime.

For years, people have been trying to explain this seemingly unexplainable case. The most common explanation is that the indoor "rain" was the result of an ice dam in the Keiffer home. Ice damming happens when warm air enters an attic space and melts on the roof, leaking water from the roof back into the attic and later, into the house.

Ice damming is most common after a snowstorm and when the temperature hovers just below freezing at night and above freezing during the day. This would certainly be possible in Stroudsburg, Pennsylvania in late February, but it doesn't explain the reported events at the pizza parlor and the jail. It also doesn't explain how the rain would stop when Decker left the room or building.

The truth is that there were at least ten documented witnesses to these events (the Kieffer's, the Van Whys, the three police officers, Pam Scrofano, David Keenhold, and William Blackburn), many of whom witnessed the events together in pairs or groups but often at different times and different locations. In other words, it would be very difficult to arrange a hoax between all these people, especially since most of them didn't know each other before the events.

So that leaves us with the possibility that Decker was controlling, or being controlled by, some psychokinetic power that we don't understand.

Or maybe Don Decker really *was* possessed by demons. Some of us may deny that evil exists, while others are adamant it lives on Earth. Maybe Don Decker's ability to make it rain is proof that evil takes on many different forms.

THE HEXAGON ON SATURN

When it comes to the solar system, humans still have quite a way to go before we even begin to approach understanding it all, or even a fraction of it, for that matter. It's only just over half a century since the Apollo 11 mission touched down on the moon, and deep space exploration since then has been unmanned for the most part.

But some of these unmanned missions have revealed some pretty interesting and unexplained mysteries about our solar system.

When the *Voyager 1 and Voyager 2* unmanned probes flew past Saturn in 1980 and 1981, respectively, they took the most detailed photographs known to humans of the ringed planet. NASA scientists took several years to examine the photographs, and in 1987 Dr. David Godfrey noticed something quite peculiar and mysterious about Saturn - its north pole was covered by a geometric hexagon pattern.

More intense examination of this hexagon, which was augmented by the unmanned *Cassini* mission's visit to the planet in 2006, revealed that it is a cloud that's relatively stable, maintaining about the same size.

Each side of the hexagon is about 9,000 miles long, approximately 18,000 miles wide, and possibly 190 miles high. Although the hexagon is constantly rotating, its longitudinal location remains nearly constant.

To give you some perspective on the hexagon's size, four Earths could neatly fit inside it!

As strange as the hexagon's appearance is, its mystery is only deepened by the lack of a hexagon over Saturn's south pole. There is also no other known, similar geometric cloud on other planets, which has led many scientists to make a career of attempting to answer this riddle.

Scientists at Oxford think they have figured out the answer. They conducted a laboratory experiment in which they rotated tanks of liquids at different speeds. The scientists created similar hexagonal shapes in their experiments, so they hypothesized that the geometric shapes form when there is a steep latitudinal gradient in the speed of the winds on Saturn's atmosphere.

Another theory is that the hexagon was caused by an anticyclonic ring, which is when a storm is surrounded by a ring of winds turning in the opposite direction.

Still, other scientists believe that the presence of a slow jet stream that moves in the same direction as Saturn's prevailing clouds create the hexagon-shaped cloud.

Scientists will continue to debate the reason for the hexagon on Saturn's north pole, but until more probes are done, or some great breakthrough is made, this is sure to remain one of science's greatest unexplained mysteries.

NATURAL FORMATION OR EVIDENCE OF ATLANTIS?

The idea of one or more lost civilizations that existed in different places on Earth in times before standard record keeping as we know it existed has propelled the human imagination since the earliest days of civilization. The Aztecs believed in a mystical land called Aztlan and the Tibetans wrote about a hidden place called Shambala. The Greeks seemed to especially like the concept of lost civilizations, writing about the lands of Hyperborea or Thule to the north.

But none of these came close to getting as much interest as Atlantis.

The idea of the lost civilization of Atlantis was first proposed by the Greek philosopher Plato in his dialogues *Timaeus* and *Critias*. Although Plato's references to Atlantis have been written off as fiction by most modern scholars, it hasn't stopped many on the fringes of academia, and even a few in the mainstream, from forwarding their ideas of what Atlantis may have looked like, and most importantly, where it was located.

Some scholars have argued that the island of Thera was Plato's Atlantis, while others believe it was Crete, which was inhabited by the Minoan Civilization from about 3500 to 1100 BCE. These are more or less mainstream positions about the existence and location of Atlantis.

But since this book is about unexplained mysteries, let's take a look at some of the less mainstream views.

Those who believe Atlantis was a more mystical place think it was somewhere in the Atlantic. Divers Joseph Manson Valentine, Jacques Mayol, and Robert Angove are said to have discovered remnants of it off the coast of the island of North Bimini, the Bahamas on September 2, 1968.

The structure that the men discovered, which came to be known as the "Bimini Wall" or "Bimini Road," is a half-mile-long line of rectangular limestone blocks that are submerged about 18 feet underwater.

Bimini Road immediately caught the attention of geologists and archaeologists because the blocks appear to be man-made, as they are noted for their right angles. And although the blocks vary in size, they are aligned in a fairly straight line. Two other linear rock features were later discovered that lie parallel to the Bimini Road, nearer to the shore.

You may be reading this and thinking, "They found some walls off the coast of the Bahamas, so what?"

The problem is that *if* these walls, or roads, were man-made it's unknown who made them, or when. The Bahamas is an archipelago that was inhabited by the Taino people in the pre-Columbian era, but they didn't have knowledge of stone working technology. The British colonized the islands in the 17th century, and although they did have stone working technology, there is no record that they built a limestone road or wall at North Bimini.

And since the shoreline of North Bimini is today more or less what it was during British colonization, there's no reason why they would have built roads or walls *into* the ocean.

So, if no known people built these structures, then we're left with only a few options to explain this mystery.

Most mainstream geologists argue that the Bimini Wall is the result of naturally occurring wear and that the ocean currents ate away at naturally placed limestone blocks until it was finally, naturally revealed in 1968. Carbon dating has also suggested that the blocks occurred naturally, but that isn't enough to convince many people.

In his controversial book *1421: The Year China Discovered America* and its accompanying documentary, *1421: The Year China Discovered America?*, amateur historian Gavin Menzies claimed that when Chinese Admiral Zheng He's fleet was in the process of circumnavigating the globe in 1421-3, it stopped at Bimini - see his 1421 hypothesis. According to Menzies, half of the fleet, under the command of Admiral Zhou Wen, was caught in a hurricane near Bimini and built the Bimini Road from beach rock and the ships' ballast as a slipway to haul damaged junks ashore for refitting and repairs of damage caused by the hurricane.

The idea that the Bimini Road was part of Atlantis can be traced back to Robert F. Marx. Although Marx was a professional diver who certainly knew the ocean, his knowledge of history and archaeological methods was not always very sound. Still, Marx was able to gather some like-minded people, such as members of the Edgar Cayce Foundation, to forward the Atlantis hypothesis.

If you're wondering who Edgar Cayce is, he was an early 20th-century mystic who developed a pseudo-history of the world in which Atlantis played a major role. He also made several predictions about the future, many of which never came to pass, but a 1938 prediction he made about Atlantis appears to have been eerily accurate.

"A portion of the temples may yet to be discovered under the slime of ages and seawater near Bimini," Cayce said. "Expect it in '68 or '69 — not so far away."

Even the biggest skeptics and doubters of Edgar Cayce and Atlantis have a difficult time writing this prediction off as a hoax, or even false. I guess that brings us back to where we started. In the end, you decide whether the Bimini Road is a remnant of Atlantis, a result of Chinese exploration or a natural rock formation.

ROMANS IN THE AMERICAS

Earlier in this book, we explored the mysterious theory of ancient and medieval Chinese visits to North America. The evidence was certainly interesting, but not necessarily compelling enough to consider the mystery solved either way. And guess what? The Chinese are not the only people who some have claimed to have visited the Americas long before Columbus.

While the Romans were fighting the Germans on their northern borders and the Parthians on their eastern border, building the Colosseum, and establishing a republic, and later an empire, some believe they also made multiple voyages to the Americas. There's no evidence to suggest they ever established permanent trading posts or military bases in the Americas, but there are a number of small artifacts that point to the potential of several Roman visits.

Most mainstream scholars dismiss the idea of Roman contact with the Americas, but a few are open to the possibility, especially in light of the evidence.

The mystery of Romans in the Americas began not long after Columbus landed, and European colonization of North America and South America began. Occasionally, people would claim to

119

have discovered Roman-era coins buried in different locations, but these were usually written off as hoaxes or the result of coins that were left behind by early modern European explorers (from the 16th century and after). But all of these supposed caches of Roman coins were suddenly taken more seriously when a small sculpture head was discovered in Mexico in 1933.

Referred to as the Tecaxic-Calixtlahuaca Head, a small terracotta head about the size of a baseball, was discovered by Mexican archaeologist Jose Garcia Payon about 40 miles northwest of Mexico City. The find was not immediately thought to be anything out of the ordinary, as the region was the center of Pre-Columbian Mesoamerican Civilization, with the Aztecs and other peoples making the area their home. These different groups all produced statuary, but a closer examination revealed that the style and the features of the figure looked like no other Mesoamerican artifact.

The facial features of the figure certainly look more European than Amerindian; especially notable is the beard.

The Tecaxic-Calixtlahuaca head came to the attention of Austrian anthropologist Robert von Heine-Geldern, who declared in 1961 that it fit the style of Roman sculpture from the 2nd century CE. Art historian Bernard Andreae concurred, but the two experts added that it could have possibly been placed there after 1492, as the excavation site where it was discovered was dated to the years 1476 to 1510 CE.

There are a number of other apparent finds of Roman artifacts in the Americas worth mentioning.

Several clay storage jars that resemble Roman amphorae were discovered in 1982 in Guanabara Bay, Rio de Janeiro, Brazil.

They were found about 15 miles offshore, in 100 feet of water, in an area about the size of three tennis courts.

More recently, a discovery in Nova Scotia has renewed the possibility of Romans in the Americas.

In 2015, treasure hunter and colorful character Jovan Hutton Pulitzer was searching for the answers to the secrets on Oak Island - which is itself of a mystery - when he claims to have discovered a Roman shipwreck off the shore. Pulitzer produced what he says were a Roman sword, a legionnaire's whistle, gold Carthage coins, part of a Roman shield, and part of a sculpture. Jovan also claimed that the find was corroborated by Latin words in the Mi'kmaq language. It should be pointed out that although some mainstream scholars agree that the artifacts are legitimate Roman pieces, they often state they could have been placed there in modern times. Also, Mi'kmaq experts disagree with Pulitzer's assessment of the Latin loanwords.

Other possible evidence of Romans in the Americas includes a hull of a ship full of Roman amphorae discovered by scuba divers off the coast of Honduras in 1972 and a cache of Roman coins found in Oklahoma in the 1950s.

Still, other evidence of Romans in North America has been found in Europe.

In 1950, an Italian botanist named Domenico Casella identified pineapples, which are native to the New World, in frescoes from Pompeii, although many art historians argued that the items in question were pinecones.

The skeptics usually have a field day when the possibility of Romans in the Americas is mentioned. They note that a number of supposed Roman artifacts have turned out to be forgeries, while the rest can be explained by collectors dropping them in modern times as a hoax, or early modern explorers and colonists simply losing their Roman-era stashes. Gold and silver have always been prized, so Roman coins continued to be held for their bullion value long after the collapse of the Roman Empire.

The amphorae discovered in Guanabara Bay are often said to be 15th or 16th-century Spanish olive jars, and the Tecaxic-Calixtlahuaca head was said to have been placed at the dig site as a joke. The story goes that an archaeological student name Hugo Moedano planted the head, but that doesn't explain where he got the artifact in the first place!

Historians also point out that it would have been difficult for Roman-era ships to make the voyage across the Atlantic Ocean. Roman ships, like most of the era, sailed close to shore and rarely ventured across the open water of the Mediterranean to get to its southern shore. It's also noted that the Romans were actually averse to naval activity and often staffed their navies with Greeks, Egyptians, Phoenicians, and other people who had a longer history of maritime culture.

With all of that said, there's still a lot of evidence that suggests the Romans *may* have visited the Americas. Future discoveries may help clear up the unexplained mystery of Roman artifacts in the Americas, but for now, it's up to you to make a decision on this one.

THE MYSTERIOUS
GOODYEAR BLIMP

If you're old enough to have gone to a major sporting event in the United States during the 1970s or remember watching them on TV at the time, then chances are you remember the Goodyear Blimp flying overhead. Well, if you did see *it*, it was actually one of many dirigibles/airships the Goodyear corporation kept in a fleet for advertising purposes. And in the 1970s, one of those dirigibles had a very strange and mysterious history.

After the Japanese attacked Pearl Harbor in 1941, the United States military believed that attacks could happen at any time along the West Coast. The government responded in many ways. Some were controversial and many would say shameful, such as interning Japanese and Japanese-Americans, while other methods were quite logical and effective, like organizing the citizens into civil defense units.

The military also came up with some innovative defense methods that combined the resources of the private and government sectors. One of these interesting partnerships was between the Goodyear corporation and the Navy. The Navy commandeered

Goodyear's "L class" of blimps, which were too small for long-distance use or any major combat operations. Blimps were more or less obsolete as weapons in World War II, but the small L class blimps were perfect for patrolling the West Coast in search of Japanese submarines.

And there were a few minor Japanese submarine attacks on the West Coast and numerous sightings, so the Navy had plenty of work to do with its L class dirigibles.

The L dirigibles were primarily used to sight Japanese naval vessels, but each was equipped with a machine gun and depth charges in case they spotted a sub.

So, that's the background, let's get to this mystery. It all began on August 16, 1942, when airship L-8 left from its base on Treasure Island, San Francisco at 6:03 a.m. on a routine coastal patrol. Onboard were 27-year-old Lieutenant Ernest DeWitt Cody and 35-year-old Ensign Charles Adams. Despite his age, it was Adams' first flight as a commissioned officer. It was also reported that aviation machinist mate Riley Hill was supposed to be on the flight, but he was ordered off at the last moment. Riley later said heavy moisture that added weight to the blimp was probably the reason he was kept at the base. Whatever the reason, luck was on Riley's side that day!

The crew of L-8 was equipped with the standard two depth charges and a .30 caliber machine gun like most other L class blimps, but the problems Cody and Adams faced that day apparently couldn't be overcome by conventional weapons.

L-8 investigated an oil slick off the Farallon Islands, radioing their position back to the base. Fishermen on a boat made visual contact with Cody and Adams as they descended to about 30 feet to investigate the oil slick.

This was the last time anyone saw or heard from the crew of L-8.

After 9 a.m., L-8 dumped ballast and deviated from its flight path, temporarily disappearing from sight, but then reappeared at 11:15 a.m. at a low elevation on the coastline at Ocean Beach. L-8 was low enough for two fishermen to grab its tie lines and attempt to pull it down. Although they were unable to corral the blimp to the ground, they got close enough to notice that no one was inside.

The ghost ship continued on over San Francisco, deflating into a "V" shape and causing quite a stir as it did. It continued to fly over the city until it ran out of air and crashed in front of a house in Daly City, just south of San Francisco.

The military and local police quickly arrived on the scene and were quite perplexed by what they found. The ignition switch was still on, as was the radio. There were still six hours of fuel left and the valves were untouched. Cody's hat was resting on the instrument panel as if he had just set it down before whatever happened...well, happened.

The machine gun and lifeboat were also intact, but two of three life jackets were missing, suggesting to Navy investigators that something happened over the ocean.

The Navy immediately conducted a land and sea search for the missing men but called it off on August 18.

An investigation was conducted, but it only seemed to raise even more questions. L-8 was not shot down and never made contact with the ocean. Investigators originally thought the two men bailed out with their life jackets on, but since the lifeboat and all three parachutes were still in the blimp that scenario wasn't very likely.

The most logical theory is that one of the men climbed out to the gondola to fix something and that the other man then went to help him when something happened that threw both into the water. The loss of weight then caused L-8 to rise and begin its mysterious flight.

The problem with this theory is that both men were apparently wearing life jackets so their bodies would likely have been found during the search or washed ashore later.

Unable to find solid answers, people began developing their own scenarios.One was that the men were captured by the Japanese and then killed after being interrogated!

Another theory is that the men were involved in some type of desertion plot, or even a love triangle. According to the latter theory, one of the men killed the other in jealousy, dumped the body in the ocean, and then flew L-8 into San Francisco. The killer then fled before the authorities arrived.

The Navy decided to go with their gondola theory and declared both men dead in 1943.

The mystery of what happened to the ghost blimp will probably never be solved, but we do know what happened to the blimp after the events of August 16, 1942. After the war, L-8 was used by Goodyear as one of its blimps that flew over events until 1982 when it was retired.

L-8 now sits in the National Naval Aviation Museum in Pensacola, Florida, so if you're interested in seeing one of aviation's greatest unsolved mysteries up close, stop in and pay the 'ghost blimp' a visit!

NUCLEAR WEAPONS
TEST OR SOMETHING
FROM ANOTHER WORLD?

The Cold War was an era of cloak and dagger, during which nations were competing for dominance by keeping and stealing secrets as well as building military arsenals. And sometimes, secrets and arsenals went hand in hand.

After the United States began to develop its nuclear weapons program, the Soviet Union raced to keep up. Eventually, the United Kingdom, France, China, India, North Korea, and Pakistan officially joined the nuclear weapons club, with Israel becoming unofficial members in the late 1960s. The Republic of South Africa also developed a small nuclear weapons program in the 1980s, which brings us to our next unexplained mystery.

On September 22, 1979, an America Vela satellite OPS 6911 detected a "double flash" in the far south Indian Ocean between the French territory of the Crozet Islands and the South African Prince Edward Islands. The Vela satellites were specifically launched in the late 1960s to detect nuclear explosions that were in violation of the Partial Test Ban Treaty of 1963, and they could

128

also detect other signs of nuclear explosions, including gamma rays, X-rays, and neutrons.

The double flash, which was first detected by technicians in the Air Force Technical Applications Center (AFTAC) at Patrick Air Force Base in Florida, indicated that it was an atmospheric nuclear explosion of two to three kilotons. The commanding officers at the base wasted little time sending the information up the chain of command to Washington.

The military brass and civilian government officials took the incident very seriously because it could have meant any number of things. It could have meant that countries that signed the Partial Test Ban Treaty, such as the Soviet Union, were reneging and testing new weapons. It may have also confirmed what many in the international believed (that Israel had nukes) or feared (that South Africa had become a nuclear power).

The US responded by testing the air near the blast for radiation and the ocean for an impact site, but nothing was found. Low levels of iodine-131, which can be a product of nuclear fission, were detected in sheep in the southeastern Australian States of Victoria and Tasmania soon after the event. Sheep in New Zealand showed no such trace. An anomalous ionospheric wave was detected by the Arecibo Observatory in Puerto Rico on September 22, but neither of those findings helped solve this mystery. They only showed that *something* happened, but what it was and who may have been behind it remained unknown.

When the US government publicly announced what it began to call the "Vela Incident," the Department of Defense admitted that it could have been a number of things, including a bomb blast, lighting, a meteor, or a solar flare.

But since this was the Cold War, the US intelligence agencies were more prone to believe the first explanation. Although the US National Security Council admitted that it had no evidence that any nation had conducted a nuclear weapon test, or that the Vela Incident was even a nuclear weapon test at all, it indicated that its strongest suspect was South Africa.

To put things into perspective, South Africa was somewhat of a pariah nation at the time. Its apartheid government was more or less at war with the communist nations of that era and many Western nations had begun boycotting South Africa in business, diplomacy, and sports by the late 1970s. It was later learned after apartheid ended in 1994 that South Africa had developed a nuclear weapons program during the 1980s.

So, the location and the fact that South Africa was relatively isolated would seem to indicate that it had conducted a nuclear weapon test that triggered the Vela satellite. But the problem with that theory is that South Africa didn't create its own first deliverable nuclear bomb until 1982.

But maybe they had a little help.

Most people who believe the Vela Incident was a nuclear weapon test argue that it was a joint Israeli-South African undertaking. Israel already had nukes by 1979 and had also developed a working military and intelligence alliance with the Republic of South Africa. In support of this theory, South African Commodore Dieter Gerhardt, who was convicted of spying for the Soviet Union, stated in 1994 that the Vela Incident was a joint Israeli-South African project known as *Operation Phoenix*.

Neither government has officially confirmed or denied this theory.

Other nuclear weapon theories revolve around a signatory to the Partial Test Ban Treaty violating the terms. Since the incident happened close to French territory, some believe France was the culprit, while others think the Soviets tried to sneak a test in under the Americans' noses.

But if the Vela Incident wasn't a nuclear explosion, what was it?

The most likely natural explanation is that it was a meteorite, possibly hitting the satellite. It could also have been the result of a solar storm, but if neither of those was the cause, there's still one more - somewhat unsettling - possibility.

Some experts have admitted that the Vela Incident may simply have been a false positive. It could just be that *nothing* significant happened on September 22, 1979, in the Indian Ocean and that the Vela satellite was defective. That's probably the scariest possible scenario because, during the Cold War when there were plenty of people ready to push the button, the last thing we all needed was for a mystery like the Vela Incident to happen.

Thankfully, nothing catastrophic came of it!

SCREAMS ON BEN NEVIS

The British Isles aren't known for particularly high peaks or mountain climbing, but the Grampian Mountains of northern Scotland attract about 100,000 people every year who attempt to climb Britain's highest peak: Ben Nevis. With a summit of 4,413 feet above sea level, and snow at its peak for most of the year, Ben Nevis has become a popular, although underrated, climbing destination.

Ben Nevis is known for its many trails up to the summit that appeals to climbers of all levels. The mountain is even the site of an annual foot race that attracts hundreds of seasoned hill runners who attempt to tackle the 8.7-mile course.

Hiking up Ben Nevis is usually grueling and can even be quite dangerous, but on February 12, 2015, for many climbers, it became mysterious.

The day began as a cold, crisp morning that seemed perfect for an ice climb up the face of the mountain. As groups were doing ice climbs, others were taking the more traditional paths to the summit, but then they all heard something that made them stop in their tracks.

The hikers, most of whom didn't know each other, all described the same horrific screams that lasted about five minutes and then suddenly ended, followed by what sounded like a woman crying.

Some climbers also claimed they heard someone yell "tight rope!" just before the screams.

Several climbers reported the screams to the Lochaber Mountain Rescue Team, which climbed the mountain to investigate but found nothing: no trace of a body, no signs of an accident - nothing!

Even after the rescue team didn't find signs of a lost, injured, or killed hiker, many still believed the eerie screams were those of someone in distress. Although Ben Nevis is no K2, it can be a dangerous climb, especially in the winter months. Rescues and injuries are common and there were four fatalities on the mountain in 1999 alone.

But in addition to the rescue team never finding any evidence of a missing hiker, there's no record of anyone missing in the area at the time.

One logical, potential explanation is that the climbers did hear something, but that it was an animal. Deer are relatively common in the area, so some argue that the sound was a distressed deer, not a human and that the predominantly urbanite population who climb Ben Nevis didn't know the difference.

This sounds like a good explanation, but climber Christopher Sleight, who was one of the ear witnesses to the screams, said he thought he "was listening to someone who had just watched a loved one - not simply a climbing partner, but a loved one - fall to their death."

That detailed description certainly doesn't sound like a deer in the throes of death. Other logical explanations include a panicked climber who perhaps embarrassed, never admitted she, or he, was the source.

Or maybe this is a case where it actually was a hoax. Sure, the climbers heard the screams, but the screams very well could have come from a prankster climber.

And then we have more supernatural explanations.

Some think the screams were a psychological trace of a past climber's bad experience on the mountain, or even the spirit of a climber who died, forever doomed to repeat the tragedy that left them on Ben Nevis.

Another supernatural explanation comes from nearby Ben Macdui, the second-tallest peak in the British Isles. According to legend, a creature known as Am Fear Liath Mòr, the "Big Grey Man," haunts the inhabitants of the mountain and all those who attempt to climb its peak. Maybe the Big Grey Man decided to take a trip over to Ben Nevis?

VOLCANOES, AN ASTEROID, OR BOTH?

Our next mystery began about 66 million years ago when the dinosaurs ruled the Earth, and most mammals were rodents. Then, quite suddenly (geologically speaking, that is), more than three-quarters of plant and animal life was wiped out on Earth, including all the dinosaurs. This event became known as the Cretaceous-Tertiary (KT) extinction event, and although scientists have known about it for quite some time, how and why it happened has been and remains a mystery. Today, many scientists believe they know what caused the KT event, but questions remain, making this one of the greatest unexplained mysteries of science.

It should be pointed out that although the KT event may have been sudden in the big picture, it actually took place over an approximately 150,000 to 200,000-year period.

Modern paleontologists first learned of this event through excavations, noticing that there was a dig level in the ground they excavated where there were no more dinosaurs, and a number of other animals, and then suddenly mammals became dominant.

Searches for answers to the KT event first brought scientists to a region in India known as the Deccan Traps. The archaeological evidence shows that a mass outpouring of lava occurred in the Deccan Traps, probably from a super volcano or several large volcanoes, over a two-to-three-million-year period, although some scholars have more recently argued that it took place over 800,000 years. The length of the eruptions isn't as important, though, as the damage they caused.

The super volcano, or volcanoes, created a giant dust cloud that killed much of the plant life on the planet, which then killed the dinosaurs.

If you were in school up through the 1980s, this is probably the theory you remember.

However, by the late 1970s, Luis Alvarez of the University of California began doubting the volcano theory. He pointed out that the KT event was accompanied by a large spike in the amount of iridium, shocked quartz, and glassy spherules on the Earth's surface.

Shocked quartz and glassy spherules may have come from volcanoes, but iridium is rare on the Earth's crust. It is very common in meteorites, though.

So, Alvarez went public with his theory in 1980, arguing that the KT event was the result of a major asteroid impact somewhere on Earth.

Alvarez's ideas didn't immediately catch on in academia and he died in 1988 just before a major discovery was made that bolstered his theory. In 1990, the Chicxulub Crater was discovered partially on the Yucatan Peninsula of Mexico.

The Chicxulub Crater is about 124 miles in diameter, partially on land but primarily in the Gulf of Mexico. It's definitely a large enough impact spot to cover the ten-mile diameter asteroid that Alvarez hypothesized hit Earth and more than big enough to cause extinction-level destruction.

An asteroid that size would have produced an "impact winter" with the same effect on plant life as a super volcano. It would have also produced a deadly mega-tsunami.

Okay, mystery solved, right?

Many paleontologists have recently said "not so fast," as the asteroid theory certainly sounds good, but it doesn't completely explain the selective extinction that took place.

Some scholars, such as J. David Archibald and David E. Fastovsky, have combined the volcano and asteroid hypotheses with the idea of marine regression, or the lowering of sea levels. This theory has been supported by Gerta Keller, who argued that the asteroid and the Deccan volcanoes acted like a one-two punch that put the dinosaurs out for the count.

The primary challenge to either or both these arguments in the gradualist theory. The gradualist theory argues that the dinosaurs became extinct over a much longer period because, unlike the mammals, they were unable to adapt to climate change.

Long-term climate change in sub-tropical dinosaur habitats gave way to conifer-dominated mammalian habitats.

Proponents of the gradualist theory point to excavations in North America as evidence. The evidence indicates that during the last ten million years of the Cretaceous, the number of dinosaur species dropped from 45 to 12, while the number of mammal species greatly increased.

Gradualists don't necessarily deny that a super volcano erupted, or that an asteroid hit the Earth about 66 million years ago, just that the dinosaurs' doom had already happened long before those events.

We're told that science will answer all of our questions at some point in the future, but as the question of the dinosaurs' demise shows, science can't always solve every unexplained mystery.

THE VANISHING VILLAGE AT ANGIKUNI LAKE

Sometimes the line between urban myth and the legitimate unexplained mystery becomes blurred, especially when a notable passage of time has occurred. What may start as a strange story or mystery has new elements added or is significantly modified over the course of many years? Eventually, it looks entirely made up and draws the attention of gleeful skeptics who are happy to write the mystery off as a hoax.

But many of these conflated urban myths still contain a kernel of an unexplained mystery.

Our next story is one such mystery. For this mystery, we travel to the Canadian territory of Nanuvut, Canada, to the desolate region of Kivalliq and the otherwise unknown Angikuni Lake. And it's actually a bit of a two-fold mystery: the mystery of the actual event and then the mystery of how the events became conflated.

The mystery begins in 1930 when a trapper from Manitoba named Joe Labelle traveled north and visited an Inuit village on the shores of remote Angikuni Lake. He found the village's six tents abandoned and the approximately 25 villagers gone without a trace. Food was hanging over the fire pits and there were unfinished shirts laid out that the women were apparently working on. Most bizarre were the seven sled dogs strewn about the camp that had died from starvation.

In 1930, Inuits would *never* leave their sled dogs for long.

Labelle reported the situation to the Northwest Mounted Police who couldn't find the missing villagers or any evidence of what happened to them. The events of this story are certainly mysterious, but the mystery deepens when you consider the sources. It turns out that the first newspaper report of the incident is lost, but the original article was picked up by Emmett E. Kelleher, who was writing for the *Danville Bee* of Virginia in November 1930. Kelleher wrote an article about the event at Angikuni Lake complete with a picture of an Inuit village.

The only problem is that the picture wasn't of the Inuit village at Angikuni Lake.

The mystery of Angikuni Lake then became dormant for nearly 30 years until Frank Edward mentioned it in his 1959 book, *Stranger than Science*, which chronicled some of the better, and lesser, known cases of the unexplained until that time. Nigel Blundell and Roger Boar then included a much more colorful account of the incident at Angikuni Lake in their 1984 book, *The World's Greatest UFO Mysteries*.

In Boar and Blundell's book, they claimed that when the Northwest Mounted Police went to Angikuni Lake to investigate the incident, they came across another trapper and his two sons who claimed to have seen brightly-lit objects flying in the skies around the same time.

Since 1984, the incident at Angikuni Lake hasn't grabbed the imagination of UFO hunters quite as much as other notable cases, but it has come up from time to time. And as the incident at Angikuni became more well-known, other theories have been advanced to explain it.

One theory is that it wasn't aliens that took the villagers away, but a Native American creature known as the Wendigo. According to folklore, wendigos are evil spirits that lurk in the forests waiting for the right time to take a person away and capture their soul.

Others have opted for more logical explanations to this mystery.

Notable skeptic Brian Dunning has examined this mystery, coming to a few different conclusions. He points out that the case apparently received enough attention from locals at the time that the Commissioner of the Royal Canadian Mounted Police (RCMP), Cortland Starnes, issued a statement about the investigation on January 17, 1931. A Mountie Sergeant J. Nelson was sent to the region to speak with traders and Inuits, learning a few interesting things in the process.

Apparently, Joe Labelle did exist, and he was a trapper and trader, but he wasn't in Nunavut at the time of the incident. Also, no one who was interviewed claimed to know about the isolated village.

This isn't to say that village couldn't have been located there at one time since the Inuit were semi-nomadic at that time, but the RCMP never mentioned finding a camp.

Dunning conducted further research and was unable to find the 1931 RCMP report or the original 1930 article that was "lost," but he did locate Kelleher's article. Dunning ultimately concluded that the story was a hoax fabricated by Kelleher.

Even if the story was fabricated by Kelleher, there are still some unanswered questions that make this an unexplained mystery. Did the 1931 RCMP report exist? Just because no official document could be found in more recent decades doesn't mean it didn't exist at one time, with it possibly being lost in the era before digital copies or even microfilm. And if the RCMP did investigate, but Kelleher fabricated the story, how is the existence of the real Joe Labelle explained? If Kelleher made up the story, which would include the "character" of Joe Labelle, why did he use the name of a real trapper and trader from Manitoba?

The unexplained mystery in this story may just be how it all became so convoluted, in which case since Kelleher is long deceased, it will never be solved. Or, just maybe, something really did make a small village of Inuit's disappear on a cold November day in 1930?

E.T.S AMONG US
IN BRAZIL?

On August 20, 1966, one of the strangest mysteries in Brazil's history began. On that afternoon a boy was flying a kite on the Vintém Hill in the city of Niterói, just outside the city of Rio de Janeiro, Brazil, when he caught the foul odor of decomposition. He did a little more searching and found the bodies of two men.

When the local police arrived a short time later, they were confused by the scene. Although many of the responding officers had dealt first-hand with murders, suicides, and accidental deaths, they could immediately tell this was something different.

The two bodies were partially covered with grass but showed no visible signs of trauma. They were dressed in suits, with raincoats over them. Strangest of all, the men were both wearing lead eye masks.

Yes, you read that correctly: Each of the men had on a *lead eye mask*.

They were described as more like lead goggles or eyeglasses, but their purpose was not immediately, or ever, determined.

Among the other strange things found at the scene were a single, empty water bottle and a bag with two wet towels. One man had Cr $4,000 on him in a pocket and the other man had Cr $157,000 in a plastic bag.

The police also found a notebook on one of the men that had the message (in Portuguese), "16:30 be at the specified location. 18:30 ingest capsules, after the effect protect metals await signal mask."

Okay, that certainly makes for the beginning of one strange mystery. So, the local police did their due diligence and investigated the matter further, but it only got stranger.

The autopsy of the bodies revealed no signs of significant trauma or violence. There were also no signs of burning or poisoning. With that said, the lack of any evidence of foul play may have been the result of the advanced decomposition of the bodies and less advanced medical technology at the time. The deaths were eventually ruled to be due to cardiac failure.

The police investigation into the men revealed they were Miguel Jose Viana (34) and Manoel Pereira da Cruz (32) of Campos dos Goytacazes, which is about 170 miles from where they were found. Based on interviews with the two men's families, as well as other witnesses, they were able to retrace their movements on their last days, but these only seemed to raise more questions.

The two men boarded a public bus together on August 17 at about 9 a.m. for Sao Paulo to purchase electronics equipment for their business. They were reportedly carrying about Cr $3 million between them. For some reason, the pair got off at Niterói at about 2 p.m. Witnesses and receipts show they then bought the raincoats and went to a bar where they bought the mineral water.

The two men were next seen by a boy at 5 p.m. on the same hill, alive, where their bodies were later found. The same boy claims he saw the two men the next day at the same spot but that they were lying down. They were presumably dead by this point.

So, that's what we know about this mysterious case. Once the news of the strange discovery started making its way through the media, there was no shortage of theories to explain the mystery, and as the years passed, the theories only became more extreme.

One of the most popular theories is that Cruz and Viana weren't Brazilians but visitors from another planet. This theory was seemingly bolstered by the fact that there was a UFO sighting in the area on August 17 and a statement by an associate of the men.

During the investigation, the name Elicio Gomes came up as a person of interest. When the police questioned Gomes, he told them that he, Cruz, and Viana were members of a spiritualist group that was attempting to communicate with aliens. Cruz and Viana were an integral part of the group due to their electronic expertise, as they built devices to send messages to space. Gomes also told police that two months before their deaths, the two men invited the spiritualist group to a beach where they witnessed a UFO fly overhead.

Some people believe this explains the words "await signal mask" in the cryptic note and that the mask possibly protected them from UFO radiation.

Did aliens get angered at the men somehow and decide to kill them? Were the pills they took somehow ineffective for alien radiation and they died? It's anyone's guess.

Most people, though, look to more terrestrial answers to this mystery.

Other theories state that the two men were involved in either criminal activity, espionage, or both.

A 1969 newspaper article stated that a female relative of Sao Paulo underworld figure Hamilton Bezani was told by three criminals with connections to the Brazilian spiritualist scene that Cruz and Viana were carrying a large amount of cash.

The four men and the woman brought Viana and Cruz to their final resting place, where Bezani forced them to take poison at gunpoint and then made off with a briefcase that had most of the money.

There were several problems with this theory, ranging from how it was reported to the veracity of the one supposed witness. Although the forced poisoning would explain why the bodies of the men didn't show any signs of trauma, one wonders why an underworld figure would even bother.

Another potential theory is that Viana and Cruz's electronics expertise came to the attention of one or more intelligence agencies. It could be that whichever side they were working for determined at some point that they were more of a liability than an asset and decided to kill them. The money the men were carrying was paid to them by an intelligence service to be paid to other agents or to be deposited somewhere, and the cryptic instructions were given by their handlers. The men possibly thought the pills were for some part of the supposed mission, but they were really the last tool used by their handlers to tie up the loose end.

But those bizarre lead masks are never explained by this or the underworld robbery theory.

It appears that we'll never know how Cruz and Viana died, or what was the purpose of those lead masks. If you think about it enough, there are probably several more explanations for the lead mask mystery...or none at all.

FACES ON THE FLOOR

Those who believe in miracles will tell you they come in all shapes and sizes. Believers have claimed they've happened on battlefields, in places of worship, and in hospitals. And in Bélmez de la Moraleda, Spain, many believe they've even happened on a kitchen floor.

This next mystery began on August 23, 1971, when Maria Gomez Camara claimed that the image of a human face appeared on the floor of the kitchen in the home she shared with her husband Juan and her son Miguel. The appearance of the face was so disconcerting for the family that Juan and Miguel destroyed the image with a pickaxe.

According to Maria, another face quickly appeared on the floor. Belmez is not a very big town, so it didn't take long for the mayor to learn of the strange occurrence. Thinking that it may be important, and since southern Spain is more religious than many other parts of Western Europe, the mayor had the section of the floor with the face sent out for study.

You'll notice that the title of this story included "faces", plural. It turns out that after the original piece of the floor was sent out for testing, new faces continued to appear in the home into the early

2000s. The faces appeared so often that Maria and her family began advertising their home as *La Casa de las Caras* (The House of the Faces) and made it into a tourist attraction.

Nothing wrong with a little capitalism, but it raised more than a few eyebrows and brought the case to the attention of skeptics around the world.

Since the faces first appeared, numerous studies have been conducted, with the most thorough one being done by the *Instituto de Cerámica y Vidrio* (Institute of Ceramics and Glass) in 1990. The scientists ran samples from two of the faces through a battery of tests, including granulometric, chemical, and mineralogical analyses. According to Manuel Carballal, who conducted the tests, no traces of paint were found.

Luis Ruiz-Noguez also studied the faces and published a 1993 article on them in the *Journal of Psychical Research*. Ruiz-Noguez believes that the faces were made by an oxidizing chemical agent, although he didn't comment on who he thought created the image.

Professional skeptics, such as Brian Dunning, more boldly claimed that the faces were a hoax and that Maria painted them for financial gain.

There are two major problems with the hoax explanation. The first is that Maria, Juan, or Miguel, or someone they knew, would have needed access to the materials and knowledge to perpetrate the hoax. Dunning wrote that the rendering was very amateurish, but it was apparently good enough for the ICV to believe it wasn't painted. Other experts have also pointed that the faces resembled a Byzantine style, and it is unlikely that

Maria or her family would have known to copy such an ancient and distinctive style.

Another strike against the hoax thesis came in 2014 when the Spanish TV show *Cuarto Milenio* did a special on the Belmez faces. The show received samples of the faces and brought them for testing to Jose Javier Gracenea, a PhD in chemical engineering, and Luis Alamancos, a forensic criminalist and chairman of the Gabinete Pericial Inpeval and director of the Spanish Institute of Applied Criminalistics.

Gracenea determined that the faces weren't painted and there was "not external manipulation" present. Alamancos provided his expertise in forgery by attempting to replicate the faces using a variety of different methods and chemicals. He was unable to do so.

So, if the Belmez faces weren't faked, that leaves very few options. One pseudo-scientific explanation is known as thoughtography, which is the ability to project an image from one's mind onto the surface of something. If you believe this explanation, then Maria had quite a bit of psychic energy!

It should be pointed out that the faces quit appearing after she died in 2004. If you don't buy thoughtography and don't think the Belmez faces were a hoax, then that leaves the possibility of them being miracles. If they were miracles, one of the first things believers in miracles will tell you is that…they're meant to remain mysteries.

A MYSTERIOUS MURDER

George Colvocoresses was a man who lived a life of turmoil, tragedy, and triumph, and eventually died a mysterious death, or so it seems. For years Colvocoresses' death has been the subject of many books, articles, and studies about bizarre anomalies and the supernatural, with many people offering their explanations about how he died. Yet there is still no consensus.

To understand the mystery of George Colvocoresses' death, we have to begin by briefly looking at his very interesting life for some clues.

George Musalas Colvocoresses was born on October 22, 1816, on the Greek island of Chios. You may think growing up on a Greek island would be the perfect scene for an idyllic childhood, but for Colvocoresses, his formative years took place during the Greek War of Independence (1821-1829).

Most of what is today Greece was at that time ruled by the Ottoman Turks, and the Greeks and Turks had by 1821 been engaged in a conflict that went back nearly 1,000 years. So, when the Ottoman forces came to the quiet island of Chios in 1822, they killed more than 50,000 of the inhabitants and took more than 50,000 away into slavery.

George's six brothers were killed while he, his mother, and his two sisters were taken, hostage. George's father bought his freedom and sent him to the United States in 1824. Although Southern and Eastern European immigrants were quite rare in the US at the time (immigrants of that area were overwhelmingly from the German-speaking kingdoms, Ireland and the British Isles, and Scandinavia), he quickly learned English and fitted in well.

Perhaps owing to his Greek heritage, Colvocoresses was naturally drawn to the sea and sailing, embarking on a career in the Navy in 1831. He quickly rose through the ranks, earning the respect of his fellow sailors who knew him affectionately as "Colvos."

Colvocoresses explored the Pacific Ocean for the Navy before the Civil War and served the Union Navy with distinction during the war, before retiring as a captain in 1867. He married twice (his first wife died in 1863) and had four children, so at the age of 55, Colvocoresses had built a nice life and had a few more comfortable years in front of him.

But then tragedy and a mystery struck on June 3, 1872.

On that evening, Colvocoresses was in Bridgeport, Connecticut preparing to visit New York City, presumably on business. The details of what Colvocoresses was going to do in New York City or how much money he was carrying aren't precisely known due to the nature of news reporting at the time.

If you think we have fake news today, things weren't much better back then! Stories were usually driven by a healthy dose of sensationalism.

It was reported that Colvocoresses was carrying about $8,000 in cash and about $80,000 in bearer bonds, although those numbers and types of assets may have been confused in the stories. Regardless of any confusion, though, Colvocoresses was likely carrying a large sum of money and/or assets.

Colvocoresses visited a restaurant for an evening meal and then stopped at a drug store to buy some paper and envelopes at around 10:35 p.m. He then headed to the docks to catch his ferry but was murdered along the way.

Witnesses reported hearing one shot from a gun, and when they rushed to the sound, they found Colvocoresses lying dead on the ground. A gun and a sword cane were on the ground next to him, and the carpet bag that contained his cash and bonds was empty on the street.

At first, it looked like a typical mugging gone wrong, but when the police investigated the body, they could find no bullet hole on Colvocoresses' coat or vest. Oddly, there was one on his shirt, however.

The most obvious question is how could this have even happened?

Were his coat and vest open, then he got shot, and then the shooter buttoned his vest and coat back up? Obviously, this doesn't seem likely, right?

The unlikelihood of this type of murder has led to some thinking Colvocoresses committed suicide.

There are no indications that Colvocoresses was depressed or having financial problems. Although he reportedly did take out a life insurance policy on himself, it was not substantial. Also, if Colvocoresses did commit suicide, he would have had to unbutton his coat and vest, shoot himself in the heart, and then rebutton the vest and coat before he died.

The fatal shot was to the heart, which would have brought death quite quickly.

This leaves another potential explanation - misreporting.

Today, we know that the news gets its fair share of things wrong, but there are often alternative news sites or bloggers there to catch it - this wasn't the case in 1872. It could simply be that George Colvocoresses was murdered or committed suicide, one report got the details wrong, and it has been reported as such ever since.

Whatever is the case, no one was ever arrested for Colvocoresses' murder.

THE SOLUTREAN
HYPOTHESIS

Earlier, the original peopling of the Americas was discussed regarding the mysterious Chachapoya people. The idea was raised that maybe the Chachapoya didn't migrate across the Bering Land Bridge when the ancestors of the other indigenous peoples of the Americas did. It's not so strange when you think about it.

We've already looked at mysteries surrounding potential Chinese and Roman visits to the Americas in the ancient and medieval periods; but what if people were coming to the Americas even earlier?

It's difficult to think that Paleolithic "cave men" could have crossed the Atlantic Ocean in boats, more than 14,000 years before Columbus, yet there are a number of legitimate scholars who point to evidence they claim proves this. The advocates of this theory - known as the Solutrean hypothesis - believe that their theory, which is on many levels quite mysterious, helps solve the mystery of the sudden appearance of the Clovis culture in North America and its similarities to the early Solutrean culture in Europe.

155

As academics debate this theory, the mystery only seems to grow.

In the 1920s, archaeologists working at sites near Clovis, New Mexico discovered unique tools that marked a distinct Paleolithic culture. Later, other sites were discovered throughout North America, leading scholars to term this the "Clovis culture," which existed from about 13,000 to 11,000 years ago.

The discovery of the Clovis culture was huge because it was shown to be the first major North American Paleolithic culture and the most advanced for the era. The discovery led to debates about how the culture formed so quickly - if it did form quickly - with many different theories being advanced.

But all scholars agreed that the distinct spear points the Clovis people made were a key to their success and what made them unique. Or, at least, that's what scholars thought...

In the early 1970s, a number of American and European archaeologists began noticing that the Clovis points looked very much like those made by the previous Solutrean culture, which existed from about 22,000 to 17,000 years ago. So, this would seem to indicate that the Solutreans were the direct ancestors of the Clovis people, right?

Well, there's one major problem with that theory. The Solutrean culture was based in France, Spain, and Portugal. The Solutrean people may have been quite advanced for the Paleolithic Period - they were, after all, the people responsible for the famous cave paintings in France and Spain - but they didn't have the ability to navigate across the Atlantic Ocean.

Or did they?

The Solutrean hypothesis states that a group of Solutrean people used navigation and survival skills similar to the modern Inuit. The Solutreans would have left France, which was on the edge of the ice pack before 17,000 years ago, in small boats and gone from ice floe to ice floe following the game. They would have collected water from melting icebergs and used seal blubber for heating oil.

After hopping across the ice floes, the Solutrean migrants would have arrived near the then-exposed Grand Banks and then proceeded overland to Clovis.

Proponents of the Solutrean hypothesis point to a number of pieces of evidence they say support their argument, in addition to the similarities between Solutrean and Clovis arrow heads.

They note that bone needles used for sewing waterproof clothing, similar to what modern Inuit use, have been discovered at Solutrean sights in Europe.

Solutrean hypothesis advocates also note that that genetic group haplogroup X2 is most heavily distributed in Anatolia and northeast North America, which would seem like an anomaly at first, but not if you consider the route the Solutreans would have taken.

The Solutrean hypothesis was at first regarded as pseudo-science or alternative history, but in more recent years has been advocated by respected scholars such as Bruce Bradley of the University of Exeter and Dennis Stanford of the Smithsonian Museum.

Most scholars still take issue with the Solutrean hypothesis, though.

Lawrence Straus of the University of New Mexico, who is one of the best-known experts on the Clovis culture, notes that there is a large gap between when the Solutrean ended and the Clovis began. He also pointed out that the Clovis culture lacked the cave art that was indicative of the Solutrean, and that many of the Clovis spear points were made with a process called bifacial fluting, which was never utilized by the Solutreans.

The genetic data has also been questioned.

Since the sample sizes used were so small, it's difficult to make sweeping assumptions about the background of entire populations, and other studies of the remains of Clovis people suggest their genetics were similar to those of other early Americans, whose DNA can be linked to Asia.

Although many are quick to dismiss the idea of the Solutrean hypothesis as lacking merit, others believe that it accurately may help answer some of the mysteries concerning Paleolithic migrations.

ARE THEY FROM OUTER SPACE?

When most of us think of the possibility of extra-terrestrial life forms visiting Earth, we tend to think of them as looking humanoid or maybe reptilian. Maybe the visitors will look more like E.T. than Luke Skywalker, but E.T. still had a humanoid form, more or less, as he had two arms, two legs, and one head.

But isn't it just as plausible that beings from another planet would look nothing at all like us? After all, if you look at all the animals on Earth, very few have humanoid appearances. If creatures did come here from another planet, they'd have to be equipped to live in extreme heat or cold, elevations and depths, and watery as well as dry environments.

If there's one creature on this planet that could fit that description, though, it would be tardigrades.

Tardigrades, also known as water bears, are several different species of eight-legged segmented animals that usually only measure about half a millimeter when fully grown.

They were first discovered under the microscope of German zoologist Johann August Ephraim Goeze in 1773, and ever since they've been one of science's greatest unexplained mysteries for a number of reasons.

The first major mystery behind the existence of tardigrades is their ability to survive in any environment. Tardigrades are found on every continent on Earth, including Antarctica, and have been observed surviving - 459 as well as 330° F, from the poles to the bottoms of volcanoes.

These mysterious little animals so perplexed scientists that they've been the subject of numerous experiments to see just how much they can take!

In 1963, French biologist Raoul-Michel May subjected a Petri dish full of tardigrades to X-rays at 500 times the lethal dose for humans, only to discover that most of them lived.

This experiment has been repeated in the decades since with similar results. Scientists were at a loss to explain why and how the microscopic creatures can handle such high amounts of radiation since it's not something they would normally encounter.

Outer space is something that tardigrades don't normally encounter either, or at least that's what scientists think, but a 2007 experiment revealed that they can survive in space as well.

In the 2007 experiment, dehydrated tardigrades (they also have the miraculous ability to suspend their metabolism and go into a sort of suspended animation) were sent into space for ten days.

They were exposed to the vacuum of space and some were also exposed to solar UV radiation. Most of those exposed to just the vacuum survived, while most exposed to the vacuum *and* radiation died.

Still, some *did* survive both, which is better than any other known animal species!

Later tests showed that tardigrades' survival rate after radiation exposure varies.

That's quite a mystery, but keep all that in mind while we look at another mysterious aspect of tardigrades. How tardigrades should be classified has been the source of controversy among biologists and brings to light the mysterious nature of these creatures' origins.

Scientists believe tardigrades are either related to arthropods (scorpions, centipedes, and other similar animals) and onychophora (velvet worms) or nematodes (roundworms and other similar parasites), but there is no consensus.

So, if we don't even know how to classify tardigrades, it's more difficult to understand what makes them able to survive in extreme environments. Recently, though, some researchers believe they've discovered the key to that mystery.

It's believed that tardigrades have a special protein that allows them to desiccate and rehydrate without damaging their cells.

The protein also enables them to go into cryptobiosis (suspended animation) for extremely long periods. Some tardigrades have even been reanimated ten years after going into cryptobiosis!

But this all brings us back to the mystery of the tardigrades' origins. Scientists have been able to trace the earliest known members of the phylum back to the Cretaceous Period (145 to 66 million years ago), but where and what they evolved from before that is still a mystery.

Some people outside the mainstream have even suggested that tardigrades aren't originally from this planet.

That's not so hard to believe when you consider all of the unexplained mysteries surrounding this tiny animal.

THE SHUGBOROUGH INSCRIPTION

If you happen to be a member of Britain's nobility and you want to see something truly strange and unexplained, take a trip to Shugborough Hall in Staffordshire to check out the cryptic Shugborough Inscription. At first glance, the monuments upon which it is written look like many others you'd find on a noble's estate. However, closer inspection reveals that this monument holds a more than 200-year-old mystery.

The monument was commissioned by owner Thomas Anson between 1748 and 1756. Anson was an amateur architect, a member of the British parliament, and part of the family that owned the hall. Anson's may hold an important clue, so we'll come back to that later.

The centerpiece of the monument is a carving done by Flemish sculptor Peter Scheemakers of French artist Nicolas Poussin's first version of the *Shepherds of Arcadia*. The scene depicts a woman and three men, with two of the men pointing at a tomb. The Latin phrase "Et in arcadia ego" ("I am also in Arcadia") is inscribed on the tomb.

But the most interesting inscription is the one below the carving.

The capital letters *OUOSVAVV* are inscribed between the capital letter "D" on the left and "M" on the right.

It's believed that the D and M represent the Latin phrase "Dis Manibus" meaning "dedicated to the shades," which was commonly used on Roman tombs. Yet the meaning of *OUOSVAVV* has perplexed people around the world — including none other than Charles Darwin - since it first became public knowledge.

Some of the theories are grounded in logic, while others veer into conspiracy theory land. Let's take a look at some of the more popular ones, beginning with the idea that the letters were simply Latin initials.

The Latin initialism explanation was first forwarded by Oliver Stonor in 1951. He believed that the letters *OUOSVAVV* were actually initials for the Latin phrase, "Optimae Uxoris Optimae Sororis Viduus Amantissimus Vovit Virtutibus" ("Best of wives, best of sisters, a most devoted widower dedicates (this) to your virtues"). Stonor argued that George Anson, the brother of Thomas, dedicated the monument to his beloved deceased wife. Anson, like all the upper class of that era, did know Latin, so it's not difficult to see him writing a Latin dedication for his wife. Some experts have noted that the grammar of the phrase is incorrect, but just because Anson knew Latin doesn't mean he was a Latin scholar!

Other Latin initialism theories have argued the letters are initials for Ecclesiastes 12:8 or John 14:6. These would also fit the era, as nobles then were also quite familiar with scripture.

But since Anson was an English noble and his first language was English, many believe the cryptic *OUOSVAVV* is a set of English initials.

Margaret the Countess of Lichfield (1899-1988) concurred with Stonor's assessment that the monument was dedicated by George Anson to his deceased wife but thought the initials were those from an English poem. Other theories have stated that they may represent the names of some of the residents at Shugborough.

The most interesting theories concerning the Shugborough Inscription are those that state it is some type of cipher or secret code. Some believe it points the way to secret treasures while others say it guards some esoteric knowledge.

One interesting theory relates to George Anson's career as an admiral in the British Navy. George Edmunds wrote in his 2016 book, *Anson's Gold*, that *OUOSVAVV* marks the precise longitude and latitude where Admiral Anson left a cache of Spanish gold. According to this theory, George Anson was unable to recover the treasure but gave the coordinates to his brother to be permanently enshrined at their family manor so that a future member of the family could recover it.

Others have also argued that the letters actually stand for numbers. For example, if all of the letters are given a Roman numeral except "U", which has no equivalent Roman numeral, the numbers can be added up to a total of 1594, the year Nicolas Poussin was born.

The often-mysterious style and subject matter of Poussin's work brought things full circle back to the Shugborough Inscription. It even led some to claim that it is evidence of a secret organization known as the Priory of Sion.

The Priory of Sion became known to the world through the 1982 book, *The Holy Blood and the Holy Grail* by Michael Baigent, Richard Leigh, and Henry Lincoln. The authors argued in the book that Jesus started a family with Mary Magdalene, moved to France, and intermarried with the French nobility and started the Priory of Sion.

The authors further argued that the *Shepherds of Arcadia* gave clues to all this.

Among the many problems with this theory is that the Priory of Sion was started in 1956 by a guy named Pierre Plantard who had, let's just say, grandiose ideas of history and himself. Unlike some of the historical mysteries we've examined in this book that have *some* mainstream scholarly support, the Priory of Sion theory for the explanation of the Shugborough Inscription has absolutely *no* followers in the academic world.

Another theory that converts *OUOSVAVV* into numbers claims the sum equals 2,810, and it just so happens that's the distance to Oak Island, Nova Scotia, where the famous Money Pit sits, waiting for treasure hunters to unlock its secrets.

Another theory circulating on the internet is that two of the "Vs" stand for the number ten, which is the total number of letters if D and M are included with *OUOSVAVV*. The theory then claims that the remaining letters are an anagram for the phrase "Devout Mason," presuming one or all of the Anson men were freemasons. The theory doesn't indicate how the letter "T" in the phrase is derived, though.

With the popularity of books and film franchises such as *The da Vinci Code* and *National Treasure*, there's little doubt that the Shugborough Inscription will continue to garner plenty of interest among amateur internet sleuths who will claim to have solved the mystery. But the reality is that unless a document is discovered that explicitly states what the inscription means, it will likely remain an unexplained mystery.

THE MYSTERIES OF THE GUANCHES PEOPLE

Our next story brings us to the Canary Islands, which is an archipelago located about 62 miles west of Morocco in the Atlantic Ocean. Today, the Canary Islands, or "Canaries" as they are commonly known, are part of Spain, but for most of their history, they have been isolated and quite mysterious.

The native people of the Canaries are known as the Guanches and they hold enough mysteries for a book, but for now let's focus on two of the biggest mysteries of this enigmatic group: their background and some incredible structures they built.

The Spanish first made contact with the Guanches people when they arrived on the Canary Island of Tenerife in the 14th century. The Spanish were perplexed by the Guanches because they spoke a language they didn't understand and wore clothing made from goat skins. The Guanches lived in caves as well as small round houses, had pottery, and liked jewelry.

The Guanches were also notably Caucasian in appearance.

The Spanish quickly conquered these Neolithic people and incorporated them into Spanish culture, but their origins remained a mystery for centuries, and elements of it remain baffling in many ways.

The most obvious question is where did the Guanches come from and when did they come to Tenerife?

The Roman historian Pliny the Elder wrote about the Canaries being uninhabited in 50 BCE but with signs of ruined buildings and monuments. Roman and Greek historians weren't always the most reliable sources, though, and modern archaeologists have suggested that the Canaries were inhabited as early as the 6th century BCE, although that doesn't mean it was the Guanches who inhabited the islands.

Modern DNA sequencing has seemingly helped solve some of the mystery of the Guanches' origins, with a 2017 study indicating that the Guanches have a similar DNA profile to the Berbers of North Africa. Although this mystery has apparently been solved, the question of the Guanches' language remains uncertain.

The only traces of the Guanches language found today is in some of the names of native Tenerife families, a few sentences, and some individual words. Although it's believed the Guanches' language was probably related to Berber, elements of it are unlike Berber.

So, the Guanches' language remains an unexplained mystery, but an even bigger mystery surrounds the Guanches' culture.

Located just outside the town of Güímar are six rectangular structures that resemble the pyramids of Mexico quite a bit - so much so, in fact, that many people have thought there must be a connection. The Pyramids of Güímar, as they are known, were much later, though, in the 19th century.

The Pyramids of Güímar, which originally numbered nine, were made from lava stone without mortar or any type of binding material. Some of the pyramids stand nearly 40 feet high, but the methods used to build them, as well as their purpose, are a mystery of history.

Most archaeologists believe the pyramids weren't planned but were instead the result of people clearing land for cultivation. As they dug up the lava stones from the ground, they carefully piled them into neat little pyramids. Since the research has shown that they were built in the 1800s, archaeologists who adhere to this theory argue they'd have no other purpose for pyramids - the Guanches were by that time part of Spain and were Christians.

In other words, the pyramids could not have been used for ceremonial purposes as they were in pre-Columbian Mexico.

But if they were just stones cleared for farming, they would be in a haphazard pile, not carefully arranged pyramids. This is what Norwegian adventurer Thor Heyerdahl argued after he visited the pyramids in 1991. Heyerdahl noted that the ground of the pyramids is level, the stones are carved, and the pyramids all have staircases. He also pointed out that the rocks were taken from some distance across the island. Heyerdahl came to the conclusion that the dating of the pyramids was wrong and that they were much older.

Heyerdahl incorporated his ideas about the Pyramids of Güímar into his wider theory that pre-Columbian peoples were in contact with Old World cultures, particularly ancient Egypt. Although Heyerdahl's ideas have not been accepted by most in academia, some academics agree that there's more to the Pyramids of Güímar than meets the eye.

The idea that the Pyramids of Güímar are older than the 19th century has little support, though. The Spanish never mentioned these structures when they first encountered the Guanches, but one could argue that they never mentioned them when they were built either...

And there *was* that reference by Pliny the Elder to ruins in the Canary Islands!

In 1991, one year after Heyerdahl proposed that the Pyramids of Güímar were somehow connected to the pyramids in Mexico, three scholars from the Canary Institute of Astrophysics offered their own unique take on this mystery. Juan Antonio Belmonte Avilés, Antonio Aparicio Juan, and César Esteban López conducted experiments at the Pyramids of Güímar that produced some interesting results.

They found that some of the walls mark the directions of the solstices. Plus, if one stands on the top of the largest pyramid during the summer solstice, one can see a double sunset. The scholars argue that it was no coincidence that the pyramids mark the solstices, but unlike Heyerdahl, who linked them to Mesoamerican cultures, the three Canarian scholars believe that the 19th-century dating is correct. The answer, they argue, is found in the esoteric ideas of freemasonry. As such, they contend that the owner of the land had the pyramids built, in line with freemason ideology.

Perhaps the biggest mystery of the Guanches is how they so quickly and quietly drifted into oblivion after they were "discovered" by the Spanish. Maybe it serves as a lesson for us moderns to always remember the past. Someday who we are, where we came from, and the things we've done will become a mystery to the people of the future.

A MYSTERY IN
THE AMAZON

The Amazon basin in South America is a vast area that's full of many mysteries waiting to be solved. A major part of the Amazon's mystique is due to its size, as it covers about 2,400,000 square miles or 35.5% of the landmass of the South American continent. Large parts of the countries of Brazil, Ecuador, and Peru are within the Amazon basin as well as parts of Colombia, Guyana, Suriname, and Venezuela. In addition to the Amazon basin's size, most of it is covered by the Amazon rainforest, which makes travel through it difficult and in some places impossible.

Deadly animals, disease, and in some places, unfriendly locals, do their best to keep outsiders away from the deepest reaches of the Amazon basin, and its hidden secrets.

But more than a few have attempted to unlock some of the region's riddles.

The most notable of these explorers was Englishman Percy Fawcett, who searched the jungles of Brazil for a lost city he called "Z", which he believed was once part of a great Amazonian civilization. The location - or even the existence of Z - remains a mystery, but in the course of the search Fawcett, his son Jack, and their friend and fellow explorer, Raleigh Rimell, disappeared in the Amazon jungle.

The disappearance of the explorers has served to make the mystery of the lost city of Z even more mysterious.

It's unknown when this mystery really began because we don't know for sure when Z was built, who built it, or if it even exists. We'll get to the potential answers to those questions later, but for now, let's look at Fawcett and the circumstances that brought him to the Amazon basin.

Fawcett was born on August 18, 1867, in Torquay, Devon, England, and received a proper, upper-class British education that put him on track for a nice career in the military as an officer. Fawcett excelled in the military, not so much because he loved war, but more so because he loved the world. Fawcett was cut from the same cloth as other explorers and adventurers of his era, who traveled the world and provided inspiration for fictional characters such as Indiana Jones.

Fawcett was particularly drawn to Brazil and the mysteries he believed were underneath the canopy of its rainforest. From 1906 to 1924, Fawcett conducted seven expeditions in Brazil, documenting his observations and making contacts with members of the indigenous tribes.

As he carried out his expeditions and talked to the indigenous people of the region, Fawcett kept hearing about a lost city in the Mato Grosso state of Brazil. Fawcett initially took such stories with a grain of salt, but eventually, he had heard so many of them - and identifying an intriguing Portuguese document in the National Library of Brazil - that he began to believe a lost city did exist.

The document Fawcett found is now known as "Manuscript 512." The Portuguese-language document, which was written by João da Silva Guimarães, relates how a group of Portuguese explorers known as *bandeirantes* discovered the ruins of a city in the Brazilian state of Bahia. The document describes the city as having Greco-Roman characteristics with hieroglyphic inscriptions. The veracity of Manuscript 512 has been questioned by scholars since it was first rediscovered at the National Library of Brazil in 1839, but Fawcett believed it was a key to finding Z.

Fawcett didn't believe the city mentioned in Manuscript 512 was *the* Lost City of Z, but he thought that they both may have been part of a greater Amazonian civilization.

So, in 1914, Fawcett was ready to embark into the Amazon to find 'Z', or evidence of it. Then World War I broke out in Europe. The discovery of Z would have to wait until the war was over, and Fawcett was a bit older.

Now we come to the two major unexplained mysteries of this story: Fawcett's disappearance and the existence of Z. We know that Fawcett and his companions left Cuiabá on April 20, 1925, on their final expedition. The team included the Fawcetts, Rimell, two Brazilian workers/guides, two horses, two dogs, and eight mules. The last communication Fawcett had with the outside world was on May 29, 1925. He wrote a letter to his wife from what they called "Dead Horse Camp" and gave it to an indigenous runner. The three Englishmen left their Brazilian workers behind and went deep into uncharted territory, never to be seen again.

Or were they?

The British Royal Geographical Society sent several expeditions to find the men but came up empty-handed every time. One searcher even died. Finally, in 1927, they were declared dead. Yet the mystery of three men's deaths just began heating up at that point.

The common theory is that the three explorers were killed by hostile Indian tribes deep in the jungle. This theory was seemingly bolstered by accounts given by Indians that they killed three or two white men in the jungle, but the accounts are also questionable since they were quite varied.

One account claimed that the Fawcetts were killed by arrows shot by tribesmen while Rimell had died of a fever. The stories also varied concerning what tribe killed them and where.

Members of the friendly Kalapalo tribe said that the three Englishmen entered hostile territory after leaving them, but that the two younger men were already sick, so illness could have been the cause of at least two of their deaths.

Those who knew Percy Fawcett, such as Henry Costin, had their own opinions on what happened. Costin had traveled with Fawcett on five previous Brazilian expeditions and was therefore relatively familiar with the territory. He said that since Fawcett had developed such a good rapport with the natives of the region, it was unlikely that the three men were killed by any tribes. It was more likely that they died of starvation, illness, or exhaustion and the jungle claimed their bodies.

Since the 1950s, there have been claims that Fawcett's bones were discovered in the jungle, but none of these claims has been confirmed with DNA evidence. As the theories of death at the hands of natives has gone nowhere, others have developed different theories.

Perhaps the most interesting, and least likely, of these alternate theories is that the men purposely joined a native tribe to live away from modern society and start a new religion. This theory - which sounds part-New Age fantasy and part 'Gilligan's Island' was advocated by TV director Misha Williams in the 2000s. As strange as this theory may sound, it isn't completely unbelievable, as Percy Fawcett's brother, Edward Douglas Fawcett, was a follower of eastern religions. The alternative religion/philosophy of theosophy was also quite popular with Fawcett's class at the time, so the theory shouldn't be completely disregarded.

Other than death at the hands of hostile natives, the other likely explanation for the men's disappearances is the simplest - they were robbed. In 1979, Percy Fawcett's signet ring turned up in a Brazilian pawnshop, suggesting that he and his party were robbed, murdered, and disposed of in a river. So, the mystery of Percy Fawcett's disappearance will likely remain so for a while, but that brings us back to the original mystery in this story - the existence and location of the Lost City of Z.

South America has been home to several advanced cultures, so the idea that an advanced civilization could have existed in the Amazon basin is not impossible. There were some Amazonian people who advanced beyond the Paleolithic tribal level.

Many modern scholars believe the stories about Z that Fawcett heard from local tribes actually referred to the archaeological site of Kuhikugu. Kuhikugu was a site of 20 towns that housed around 50,000 people at its height before it was probably wiped out by disease brought by the Europeans.

Several centuries before Fawcett, 16th-century Spanish explorer Francisco de Orellana reported dense indigenous population centers in the Amazon basin, but no great stone monuments or cities of stone.

It should be pointed out that the Amazon basin would not be the prime location for a city made of stone for a number of reasons. Primarily, stone is not common in the rich alluvial soil and transporting it there, from stone rich regions, such as the Andes, would have been quite difficult.

With that said, it doesn't mean that the people of the Amazon basin couldn't have built a city of stone that's waiting to be found by a new generation of intrepid explorers.

WHERE'S DUTCH'S FORTUNE?

The 1920s is commonly known as the Roaring 20s, at least in the United States. Doughboys had just come back from Europe, there was a real estate boom, and new technologies, such as radios, telephones, and automobiles were becoming more affordable and common.

But the 1920s was also the era of Prohibition in the US (1920-1933), which created a situation where there was a lot of money circulating and few places where disposable income could be spent.

Enter the gangsters of the National Crime Syndicate.

Comprised of primarily Italian and Jewish gangsters like Al Capone, Meyer Lansky, and Charles "Lucky" Luciano, different Syndicate factions took control of alcohol bootlegging and sales across the country, making millions in the process. Among the gangsters who earned millions in a relatively short period of time was Arthur Simon Flegenheimer.

Chances are you've probably never heard of Flegenheimer, but you may have heard of his better-known street name, Dutch Schultz.

Schultz/Flegenheimer was born in 1901 to German-Jewish immigrant parents in New York City. Things were tough back then for young Arthur and only got tougher when his father left the family. Arthur did a number of legitimate jobs to support the family but eventually drifted into the tough life of early 20th-century New York City ethnic street gangs. It was while he was in his teens that he began going by Dutch Schultz, although it's disputed why or how he took that name. Some say he took it in homage to a local gangster while others believe it was related to a legitimate job that he had working for the Schultz Trucking Company.

Either way, "Dutch Schultz" sounded a bit tougher and less Jewish than Arthur Flegenheimer, although the core of his criminal associates throughout his short life was Jewish.

By the late 1920s, Schultz had amassed a small criminal empire in Manhattan. Schultz had his hand in gambling, extortion, sex work, and contract murder, and he was protected by an army of corrupt police, judges, and public officials. It's estimated that Schultz was making about $20 million a year - yes *million*, in 1920s dollars.

And since Schultz, like many gangsters of his era, refused to use traditional banks the question of where his fortune is now has become an unexplained mystery.

We know that Schultz liked to live the good life but when he was murdered in 1935, he was only 34 years old, with no legal wife or children, leaving plenty of money left in his fortune that's never been recovered. Hopefully, a closer look into the events in Schultz's life leading up to his murder may help solve this mystery.

When federal income tax became law under the Sixteenth Amendment of the United States Constitution in 1913, it gave the government new tools to go after criminals such as Dutch Schultz. Due to their influence with local and state law enforcement and officials, as well as their ability to intimidate jurors, gangsters of this era were able to beat most county and state charges, but the IRS (known at the time simply as the "Revenue Service") worked by different rules.

In the 1930s, US Attorney Thomas Dewey made it his mission to go after the gangsters of New York. Since they often covered their tracks in the ways described above, he opted to use tax evasion as a way to bring them to justice.

Schultz was charged and indicted for tax evasion in 1933 and went on trial in 1934. The trial ended in a hung jury and in a second trial Schultz won an outright acquittal in 1935.

But things were touch and go for a while for Schultz, and it looked like he would be headed for an extended stay in Alcatraz - maybe even in a cell next to Capone. As Schultz attended his first trial in Syracuse, New York and his second trial in Malone, New York - both upstate cities - it's believed by many that he buried his fortune somewhere in the Catskill Mountains, just in case he ended up behind bars.

According to rumors, Schultz met with two of his most trusted men - Marty Krompier and Bernard Rosenkrantz - in a safehouse in Connecticut where they packed bundles of thousand-dollar bills, negotiable Liberty Bonds, gold and silver bullion and coins, diamonds, gems, and other jewelry into a strongbox. Schultz and Rosenkrantz then drove over to the Catskills near Phoenicia, New York where they buried the cache.

The loot was estimated to be worth $7 million at the time or about $132 million today!

Schultz never got to enjoy that cache. The Syndicate decided that he was too much of a loose cannon and ordered a hit on him. On October 23, 1935, two Syndicate hitmen entered Schultz's hangout, the Palace Chop House in Newark, New Jersey and began firing on Schultz and his crew. Schultz was shot and died from his wounds a day later. Rosenkrantz also died in the Palace Chop House shootout but Krompier was at another location.

Although Krompier wasn't with Schultz and Rosenkrantz when they buried the treasure, legend has it that Rosenkrantz told him where it was and even drew him a map. Rosenkrantz informed Krompier that Schultz even marked the location of the cache by carving an "X" on a nearby tree.

So, if you're ever in Phoenicia, New York and decide to do a little hiking, make sure to look carefully at all the trees - you may help solve a mystery and become a millionaire in the process!

DID COLUMBUS SEE
A SEA MONSTER?

You likely know something about explorer Christopher Columbus who was born in Genoa, Italy; how he opened up the New World for the Spanish crown and began the wave of exploration and colonization that helped make the Americas what they are today. Those are well-known facts, as are *most* of the elements of Columbus' life, but three events took place during his voyages to the Americas that have become unexplained mysteries.

The first two events took place on Columbus' first voyage to the Americas in 1492, while the third took place during his second voyage in 1494. The first two events were potential UFO sightings, while the third was...well, I think that one will speak for itself.

Before we get to the mysteries, it's important to point out how we know about them in the first place. There wasn't photography any kind of voice recording technology, or even typewriters in the 1400s, so all documentation was done with a quill and ink on paper. Columbus apparently did keep a diary and a logbook of his journeys from August 3, 1492, to March 15, 1493, but the original is lost. Thankfully, Spanish bishop and historian, Bartolomé de las Casas (1484-1566), made a copy of the important document in Spanish that became known as the *Diario* ("Diary"), which was later translated into several different languages.

The other primary source of Columbus' voyages and the third mystery surrounding the explorer's life is the biography written by his son, Ferdinand "Fernando" Columbus (1488-1539). The book was originally written in Spanish, then translated into Christopher Columbus' native Italian, before being translated into dozens of modern languages. The title goes by different names in English, with many being sold simply as *The Life of Christopher Columbus*. Ferdinand accompanied his father on his fourth and final trip to the New World that left Spain on May 9, 1502. He returned to Spain on November 7, 1504. It was a tough journey for a 13-year-old to make, as the explorers faced hostile Indians, diseases, mutiny, and a lack of cooperation from the Spanish crown. Christopher died on May 20, 1506, and within a few years, Ferdinand began writing his biography based on his personal observations as well as information related to him from the elder Columbus and those who knew him.

The background of these two books will be important when we consider the veracity of these three mysteries.

According to the *Diario*, the first unexplained occurrence took place on September 15, 1492.

"They sailed that day and night 27 leagues and a few more on their route west. And on this night, at the beginning of it, they saw a marvelous branch of fire fall from the sky into the sea, distant from them four or five leagues."

This passage obviously sounds like the explorers witnessed a comet or meteorite pass through the sky, but some think they saw something else. Europeans in 1492 were a lot less superstitious than is commonly believed; it was, after all, the Renaissance. Meteorite falls had taken place in Europe - most notably there was one in Ensisheim, Alsace while Columbus was in the New World - so they weren't unknown, although what they actually were wasn't understood at the time.

The issue of mistranslation has also been raised concerning this passage. Those who believe it describes something from another galaxy point out that the phrase "into the sea" can also be translated as "out of the sea."

Personally, I think they saw a meteorite, but the next light sighting reported in the *Dairio* is even stranger.

According to the account, Columbus and his crew witnessed this event on October 11, 1492, four hours before they sighted land.

"After sunset he (Columbus) steered on his former course to the west. They made about 12 miles each hour and, until two hours after midnight, made about 90 miles, which tis 21 leagues and a half. And because the caravel Pinta was a better sailor and went ahead of the Admiral it found land and made the signals that the Admiral had ordered. A sailor named Rodrigo de Triana saw this land first, although the Admiral, at the tenth hour of the night, while he was on the stern-castle, saw a light, although it was something so faint that he did not wish to affirm that it was land. But he called Pero Gutierrez, the steward of the king's dais, and told him that there seemed to be a light, and for him to look: and thus he did and saw it. He also told Rodrigo Sanchez de Segovia,

whom the king and queen were sending as veedor [inspector] of the fleet, who saw nothing because he was not in a place where he could see it. After the Admiral said it, it was seen once or twice; and it was like a small wax candle that rose and lifted up, which to few seemed to be an indication of land."

Many believe that this passage indicates they were seeing some strange light over the middle of the ocean. Although they were within hours of making it to land, the passage states they weren't there yet, so the light couldn't have been a fire on land, right?

Skeptics have argued that since Columbus and his men were passing into what was at the time uncharted territory, they didn't exactly know where they were. They may have been passing the Florida Keys and simply not known land was so close.

But that doesn't explain how or why the light they saw "rose and lifted up," does it?

The final strange thing reportedly seen by Columbus is also my favorite. According to Ferdinand, in September 1494, during Columbus' second voyage, the Admiral and several of his men witnessed something strange swimming in the sea.

"Holding on their course, the ship's people sighted a large fish, big as a whale, with a carapace like a turtle's, a head the size of a barrel protruding from the water, a long tail like that of a tunny fish, and two large wings. From this and from certain other signs the Admiral knew they were in for foul weather and sought a port where they might take refuge."

The description given of this sea creature is like nothing known, which has led to many different explanations of this mystery.

The most obvious explanation is that the men did see something, probably a whale, and they simply exaggerated the sighting or didn't understand what they saw.

The problem with that explanation is that these men were seasoned sailors who had seen plenty of whales and other creatures of the deep. Ferdinand's account was also not prone to exaggeration and because this account was so strange, it stands out from the rest.

Other scientific explanations include the effects of the light and water creating an optical illusion or that they actually did see a large sea turtle. But again, European sailors would have seen sea turtles before this journey because the leatherback sea turtle is native to the North Atlantic Ocean and the Mediterranean Sea.

And the description only said it had a body (carapace) like a turtle.

That leaves any number of explanations. Some think the description sounds a lot like a plesiosaur, while others believe it was some yet unknown animal species. Personally, I like the idea that Columbus spotted a genuine sea monster in the Atlantic!

CONCLUSION

Our universe is a vast, ancient place, so it shouldn't be a surprise that it's full of plenty of mystery. In *The Big Book of Unexplained Mysteries*, we profiled a collection of some of the more interesting science, history, true crime, supernatural, and other unexplained mysteries known.

We examined some legends of lost treasure that may or may not be out that waiting to be found.

We took a look at some alternate historical theories that have enough evidence to make even some mainstream historians take note.

We questioned some true crime cases with twists that were as bizarre and unexplainable as anything you'd find in a novel or movie.

And we looked at plenty of science wonders, from questions about animal biology to sounds and sights that can't be explained.

I'm sure you had as much fun reading these 43 stories as I did when researching and writing about them, but even more, I hope they got you thinking about our world. Our world is full of many mysteries and even if some of the ones we profiled in this book are solved, or even partially solved, many more mysteries will take their place. I'm sure there's probably a mystery or two you remembered while you read this book, so keep thinking of them and look forward to future volumes where we explore more unexplained mysteries of our world.

Made in the USA
Las Vegas, NV
15 December 2023

82945794R00108